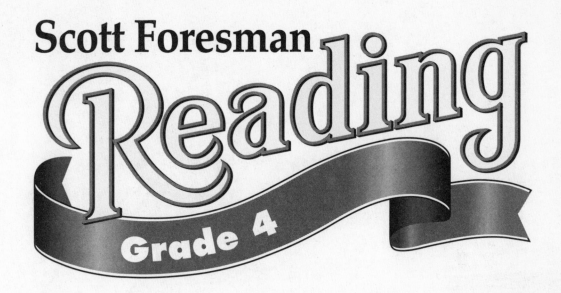

Scott Foresman
Reading
Grade 4

Grammar
Practice Book

Scott Foresman

Editorial Offices: Glenview, Illinois • Parsippany, New Jersey • New York, New York
Sales Offices: Reading, Massachusetts • Duluth, Georgia • Glenview, Illinois
Carrollton, Texas • Ontario, California

Editorial Offices
Glenview, Illinois • Parsippany, New Jersey • New York, New York

Sales Offices
Reading, Massachusetts • Duluth, Georgia • Glenview, Illinois
Carrollton, Texas • Ontario, California

ISBN 0-328-00667-X

11 12 13 14 15 16 17 18 – DBH – 06 05 04 03

Table of Contents

Unit 3 Verbs

Name_____

Statements and Questions

REVIEW

Directions: Write **S** if a group of words is a statement. Write **Q** if it is a question.

_____ **1.** Do you have a pet?

_____ **2.** What kind of pet do you have?

_____ **3.** Cats and dogs are the most common pets.

_____ **4.** Pets can be fun.

_____ **5.** Pet owners also have many responsibilities.

_____ **6.** Proper pet care takes time, effort, and money.

_____ **7.** Do you feed and exercise your pet every day?

_____ **8.** When did you last brush your cat or dog?

_____ **9.** Do you know the signs of a sick pet?

_____ **10.** Libraries have many books on pet care.

Directions: Add a word or a group of words to complete each sentence or question.

11. The pet I want _____.

12. How do you know _____?

13. I would make sure _____.

14. My pet would _____.

15. What animal do you _____?

Notes for Home: Your child identified and wrote statements and questions. *Home Activity:* Take turns asking each other some simple questions and answering them using complete statements.

© Scott Foresman 4

Sentences

A **sentence** is a group of words that tells, asks, commands, or exclaims. It begins with a capital letter and ends with a punctuation mark. You can tell whether a group of words is a sentence by checking to see if it expresses a complete thought.

Sentence: My grandpa lives on a ranch.

Not a sentence: Lives on a ranch.

Directions: Read each group of words. Write **S** if it is a sentence. Write **NS** if it is not a sentence.

_____ **1.** Making the bed.

_____ **2.** Washing the dishes.

_____ **3.** My grandpa taught me to enjoy cleaning.

_____ **4.** In the kitchen.

_____ **5.** I like folding my clothes.

Directions: Choose the group of words in ( ) that will complete each sentence. Write the complete sentence on the line.

6. _____ helps your family.   (All your hard work/Makes the bed)

_____

7. Do you do _____?   (in the house/chores at home)

_____

8. Which chores _____?   (the dirty dishes/should you do)

_____

9. Someday I will have _____.   (house a mess/my own house to clean)

_____

10. A clean house _____.   (is a happy house/without any dirt)

_____

Notes for Home: Your child identified groups of words that make complete sentences. *Home Activity:* Talk with your child about an event that occurred at school. Have him or her describe the event, using complete sentences.

© Scott Foresman 4

Sentences

Directions: Match each group of words on the left with a group of words on the right to make a sentence that makes the most sense. Write the matching letter on the line.

_____ **1.** Have you ever gone   **a.** pancakes in the morning.

_____ **2.** Wonderful things   **b.** the breakfast dishes.

_____ **3.** First, we made   **c.** to visit your grandpa?

_____ **4.** Then we washed   **d.** made the beds.

_____ **5.** After doing the dishes, we   **e.** may be waiting for you at your grandpa's house.

Directions: Add a word or group of words to complete each sentence. Write the complete sentence on the line.

6. _____ make my bed.

_____

7. The wrinkled shirt _____.

_____

8. The house _____.

_____

9. My grandfather cleans _____.

_____

10. Everyone _____.

_____

Write a Paragraph

Do you help with cleaning and other chores at home? On a separate sheet of paper, describe any tasks or chores that you do. Use complete sentences.

Notes for Home: Your child practiced completing sentences. **Home Activity:** Together, make a "To Do" list of chores that need to be done. Be sure to use complete sentences.

Name _____

Sentences

Look at the picture. Then underline the word group that describes it best.

All of the sheep.

All of the sheep are eating grass.

Is eating grass.

Did you underline the second group of words? It expresses a complete thought. It is a sentence.

A **sentence** is a group of words that tells, asks, commands, or exclaims. It begins with a capital letter and ends with a punctuation mark.

Directions: Underline the group of words in each pair that is a sentence.

1. The small brown cow.   The cow grazed in the pasture.

2. Frogs caught flies.   Their stomachs with insects.

3. Many bears in the cave.   Did one bear eat fresh fish?

4. A raccoon got into our tent.   Eating all our food.

Directions: Write complete sentences. Add your own words to each word group.

5. many bears

_____

6. one grasshopper

_____

7. chased a zebra

_____

 Notes for Home: Your child identified and wrote complete sentences. *Home Activity:* Talk with your child about what you did today. Have him or her summarize your day, using complete sentences.

Name _____

Sentences

Directions: Read the word group each animal is saying. Write each word group that is a sentence.

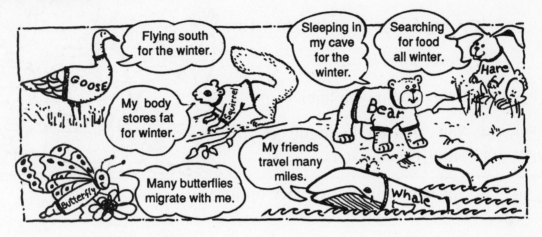

1. _____

2. _____

3. _____

Directions: Underline each word group that is not a sentence. Add words to write a sentence of your own.

4. Many birds travel south.

5. Build nests.

6. Some animals migrate to warm climates.

7. Gray squirrels.

8. need food in winter.

9. _____

10. _____

11. _____

Notes for Home: Your child identified and wrote complete sentences. ***Home Activity:*** Have your child write five sentences about his or her favorite subject in school. Remind your child to use complete sentences.

Sentences

Directions: Read each group of words. Write **S** if it is a sentence.
Write **NS** if it is not a sentence.

_____ 1. A big family has many benefits.

_____ 2. Never lonely.

_____ 3. Lots of help with homework.

_____ 4. You can meet the friends of your
brothers and sisters.

_____ 5. Someone will always stick up for you.

Directions: Add a word or group of words to complete each sentence. Write the
complete sentence on the line. Remember to begin each sentence with a capital
letter and end each one with a punctuation mark.

6. have fun together

_____

7. younger brothers and sisters

_____

8. share toys and games

_____

9. never quiet

_____

10. have responsibilities

_____

Notes for Home: Your child identified and wrote complete sentences. *Home Activity:* Choose
a picture in a magazine. Have your child write several sentences about the picture. Check that
each sentence begins with a capital letter and ends with a punctuation mark.

Subjects and Predicates

The **subject** is the word or group of words about which something is said in the sentence. The **predicate** is the word or group of words that tells something about the subject. All the words in the subject are called the **complete subject.** All the words in the predicate are called the **complete predicate.**

<u>All my friends</u> <u>love baseball</u>.

The **simple subject** is the main noun or pronoun in the complete subject. It may be more than one word. The **simple predicate** is the verb in the complete predicate. Some simple predicates can be more than one word.

<u>Peter Jones</u> <u>hit</u> the ball hard. The <u>fans</u> <u>were cheering</u> loudly.

Directions: For each sentence, underline the complete subject once and underline the complete predicate twice.

1. A.J. is always picked last for baseball games.

2. The team captains pick all the best players first.

3. A.J. waits in the hot sun.

4. I may be team captain one day.

5. My friend A.J. will not be picked last then.

Directions: For each sentence, underline the simple subject once and the simple predicate twice.

6. I had a big surprise yesterday.

7. Ms. Martin chose A.J. as a team captain.

8. A.J. made many picks.

9. Believe it or not, I was the last one picked.

10. Suddenly, I have changed my mind about picking A.J.!

Notes for Home: Your child identified simple and complete subjects and simple and complete predicates in sentences. *Home Activity:* Ask your child to identify simple and complete subjects and predicates in a variety of sentences from a story or newspaper.

© Scott Foresman 4

Name_____

Subjects and Predicates

Directions: For each sentence, underline the complete subject once. Underline the complete predicate twice. Circle the simple subject and the simple predicate.

1. Trains were slower a hundred years ago.

2. The earliest models took a long time to get anywhere.

3. A family had no other good way to travel.

4. Cars were a new invention.

5. Few people had them.

6. Our lives were much slower then.

7. Many people traveled to see new places.

8. They liked to get off at a stop and look around.

9. Most families thought cross-country travel was amazing.

10. They tried to imagine faraway places.

11. Most people never went far from home.

12. Fancy new cars had changed people's ideas about travel.

13. They made it easier to travel farther and faster.

14. Roads were appearing everywhere.

15. Trains became less important.

Write a Letter

Imagine you're traveling somewhere on a train. On a separate sheet of paper, write a letter home, describing what you see. Identify the simple and complete subjects and predicates in each sentence.

© Scott Foresman 4

Notes for Home: Your child identified simple and complete subjects and predicates. **Home Activity:** Start with a sentence that has a simple subject and predicate. Take turns adding words to make the sentence longer, without losing the starting words or idea.

Subjects and Predicates

Read the sentence about Ana. Then answer the questions.

Ana plays ball.

1. Write the one word that tells who the sentence is about. _____
That word is the subject of the sentence.

2. Write the words that tell what Ana does. _____
Those words are the predicate of the sentence.

A sentence has two parts. The **subject** is the word or group of words about which something is said in the sentence. The **predicate** tells about the subject.

Directions: Complete each sentence. Add a subject or a predicate from the lists.

Subjects	**Predicates**
You	make puppets for children
People in ancient times	are popular today

1. Puppet shows _____ .

2. Some adults _____ .

3. _____ can give your own puppet show.

Directions: Underline the subject and circle the predicate in each sentence.

4. Some children make puppets from old socks.

5. They put the socks on their hands.

6. Their fingers make the puppet move.

7. Some of the puppets look like real people.

8. Other puppets are very unusual.

9. This puppet wears a tall hat.

Notes for Home: Your child identified and wrote subjects and predicates of sentences. *Home Activity:* Look at a magazine or newspaper article with your child. Have him or her underline the subjects and circle the predicates of five sentences.

Subjects and Predicates

Directions: Draw a line between the subject and the predicate of each sentence. Then write each simple subject and simple predicate below the correct heading.

1. Many people live in Colorado.

2. The state has many mountains.

3. Few trees grow on the mountaintops.

4. The tall mountains are beautiful.

Simple Subjects	**Simple Predicates**
1. _____	1. _____
2. _____	2. _____
3. _____	3. _____
4. _____	4. _____

Directions: Read each sentence. Draw one line under the subject. Draw two lines under the predicate. Circle the simple subject and the simple predicate.

5. Many hikers climb the mountains.

6. The water in the streams is clear.

7. The birds in the trees sing in the morning.

8. Squirrels run around the trees.

9. Groups of campers look for campsites.

Write a Speech

On a separate sheet of paper, write a speech about your state. Use complete sentences to communicate your ideas.

© Scott Foresman 4

Notes for Home: Your child wrote subjects and predicates of sentences. *Home Activity:* Provide your child with two subjects. (For example: *The huge basketball, My jeans*) Have him or her make up predicates to go with the subjects and write the complete sentences.

Sentence End Punctuation

Directions: Add the correct punctuation mark at the end of each statement or question.

1. How many instruments are in a standard orchestra _____

2. Usually most orchestras have about 100 instruments _____

3. An orchestra is made up of four groups of instruments _____

4. Do you know what they are _____

5. The groups of instruments are strings, woodwinds, brass, and percussion_____

6. What is the most common string instrument _____

7. The violin is the most common string instrument_____

8. Some orchestras have as many as 36 violins _____

9. Can you name another string instrument _____

10. Yes, a harp is a string instrument _____

Directions: Write five sentences—four statements and one question. Write about a musical instrument you play or would like to play. Remember to begin each sentence with a capital letter and end each one with the correct punctuation.

11. _____

12. _____

13. _____

14. _____

15. _____

Notes for Home: Your child identified the correct end punctuation for sentences and wrote sentences. **Home Activity:** Say a statement or ask a question about music your child enjoys. Have him or her tell what punctuation mark should go at the end of each sentence.

Declarative and Interrogative Sentences

A sentence that tells something is a statement. It ends with a period. Another name for a statement is a **declarative sentence.**

I play in the orchestra at school.

A sentence that asks something is a question. It ends with a question mark. Another name for a question is an **interrogative sentence.**

Does your school have an orchestra?

Directions: For each sentence, add the correct end punctuation. Then write **D** if the sentence is declarative. Write **I** if it is interrogative.

1. Do you play a musical instrument _____ _____

2. How well do you play _____ _____

3. The violin is a beautiful instrument _____ _____

4. It isn't easy to play a violin _____ _____

5. It is important to practice every day _____ _____

6. Which musical instruments do you like _____ _____

7. You could play more than one kind of instrument _____ _____

8. Playing an instrument can make you feel proud _____ _____

9. Would you like to play in a concert _____ _____

10. Would you like to listen to some music _____ _____

11. There are many different types of music _____ _____

12. Some people don't listen to music _____ _____

13. Your family could listen to music together _____ _____

14. Everyone in my family likes music _____ _____

15. Does music make you happy _____ _____

Notes for Home: Your child identified declarative and interrogative sentences. *Home Activity:* Take turns making statements or asking questions about songs that you have listened to together.

© Scott Foresman 4

Name_____

Declarative and Interrogative Sentences

Directions: For each sentence, add the correct end punctuation. Then write **D** if the sentence is declarative. Write **I** if it is interrogative.

1. Will the orchestra start to play _____ _____

2. The audience is eager to hear the musicians play _____ _____

3. The music is soft and beautiful _____ _____

4. How long do you think the concert will last _____ _____

5. I am glad that we came tonight _____ _____

Directions: Change each of these declarative sentences into an interrogative sentence. Be sure to use the correct end punctuation.

6. The orchestra played a piece by Beethoven.

_____

7. The drums are loud.

_____

8. The violin player can play very high notes.

_____

9. There is another concert next week.

_____

10. We should go again.

_____

Write Questions

On a separate sheet of paper, write three questions about a musical instrument you like. Then answer each question with a declarative sentence.

Notes for Home: Your child changed statements (declarative sentences) into questions (interrogative sentences). *Home Activity:* To practice asking questions and making statements, take turns "interviewing" one another.

© Scott Foresman 4

Declarative and Interrogative Sentences

Read the interrogative sentence below.

1. What do you like to ride?

Write a declarative sentence. Complete the statement below.

2. I like to ride _____ .

A **declarative sentence** makes a statement. It begins with a capital letter and ends with a period. An **interrogative sentence** asks a question. It begins with a capital letter and ends with a question mark.

Directions: Decide what kind of sentence each one is. Draw a line from the sentence to **declarative** or **interrogative.**

1. His airplane just landed.   declarative
   Who was the pilot?   interrogative

2. Will he rent a car?   declarative
   He can take a taxi to the boat.   interrogative

3. I will ride my bicycle to the dock.   declarative
   How far away is it?   interrogative

Directions: Underline the capital letter. Write the correct punctuation mark at the end of each sentence. Then write each sentence correctly.

4. The man is going to the airport _____

_____

5. Will he arrive on time _____

_____

Notes for Home: Your child identified and wrote declarative and interrogative sentences. *Home Activity:* Have your child write one declarative sentence and one interrogative sentence and explain to you the difference between them.

© Scott Foresman 4

Declarative and Interrogative Sentences

Directions: Write each sentence under the correct heading. Begin each sentence with a capital letter. Use periods and question marks correctly.

1. plains are grassy lands

2. are there trees on the plains

3. do crops grow on these lands

4. cows graze on the plains

Declarative Sentences

_____

_____

Interrogative Sentences

_____

_____

Directions: Change each sentence to the kind named in ( ).

5. Our country has flat land. (interrogative)

_____

6. Do wheat fields grow here? (declarative)

_____

7. Is this the Central Plains? (declarative)

_____

Write Sentences

On a separate sheet of paper, write interrogative sentences about your town or city. Write declarative sentences to answer your questions.

Notes for Home: Your child identified and wrote declarative and interrogative sentences. *Home Activity:* Have your child write four interrogative sentences—sentences that ask questions—and give them to you to answer.

© Scott Foresman 4

Subjects and Predicates

Directions: For each sentence, underline the complete subject once and the complete predicate twice.

1. Many pictures in a museum tell wonderful stories.

2. Pictures of things in nature are called *landscapes*.

3. Most paintings like these include water and trees.

4. Portraits show lifelike pictures of people.

5. I saw one that was a portrait of the artist's dog!

Directions: Write sentences that include the following simple subjects and predicates. Remember to begin each sentence with a capital letter and end each one with a punctuation mark.

6. I   enjoy

_____

7. museums   look

_____

8. painters   use

_____

9. people   will pay

_____

10. Mrs. Andrews   studied

_____

Notes for Home: Your child identified and used complete and simple subjects and predicates.
Home Activity: Ask your child to point out the simple subject and predicate in several sentences that you find in a book, on a cereal box, or in a newspaper.

Imperative and Exclamatory Sentences

A sentence that tells someone to do something is a command, or an **imperative sentence.** It usually begins with a verb. The subject of the sentence (*you*) is not shown, but it is understood. Imperative sentences end with periods.

Don't get wet. Please take an umbrella along.

An **exclamatory sentence** shows strong feeling or surprise. It ends with an exclamation mark.

What a day for walking the dog!

Directions: For each sentence, add the correct end punctuation. Then write **I** if the sentence is imperative. Write **E** if it is exclamatory.

1. Don't take too long getting ready _____ _____

2. What a wonderful day to go to a museum _____ _____

3. Leave your umbrella here _____ _____

4. That's some big painting _____ _____

5. Please follow the tour guide _____ _____

Directions: Change each of these sentences into a command. Write your new sentence on the line. (Hint: You will not use all the words in each sentence.)

6. My art teacher says to try your best. _____

7. He says we should work in pairs. _____

8. I tell my partner to let me do some. _____

9. I tell my partner to keep helping me. _____

10. My partner tells me to be quiet. _____

Notes for Home: Your child identified imperative and exclamatory sentences. *Home Activity:* To practice using commands and exclamations, make up funny dialogue in which one bossy character gives many orders that other characters don't like.

Imperative and Exclamatory Sentences

Directions: For each sentence, add the correct end punctuation. Then write **I** if the sentence is imperative. Write **E** if it is exclamatory.

1. Let's learn to draw _____ _____

2. Please be patient _____ _____

3. I am *not* impatient _____ _____

4. Please get some paper and a pencil _____ _____

5. Watch what I do _____ _____

6. Start with an outline of the face _____ _____

7. Draw the nose next _____ _____

8. Try going a little slower _____ _____

9. Please get the brown pencil _____ _____

10. Let me help you do that _____ _____

11. How wonderful it turned out _____ _____

12. I'm so excited about your drawing _____ _____

13. Please draw a picture of me _____ _____

14. Use all your talent _____ _____

15. What fun we'll have _____ _____

Write a Memo

Imagine you're in charge of getting a big mural made for school. On a separate sheet of paper, write a memo that uses commands and exclamations and gives your friends instructions about how to get the job done.

Notes for Home: Your child decided whether sentences were commands or exclamations. *Home Activity:* Name a strong feeling. Have your child make up an exclamatory sentence to match the feeling. Name a task. Have your child make up a command to tell someone to do it.

Name_____

Imperative and Exclamatory Sentences

RETEACHING

Look at the picture. Then follow these instructions.

1. Circle the end marks of each sentence in the picture.

2. Circle the command. It is an imperative sentence.

3. Underline the sentence that shows strong feeling. It is an exclamatory sentence.

An **imperative sentence** gives a command or makes a request. It begins with a capital letter and ends with a period. An **exclamatory sentence** shows strong feeling. It begins with a capital letter and ends with an exclamation mark.

Directions: Circle each imperative sentence. Underline each exclamatory sentence.

1. Pour water on the soil.

2. Find the seeds.

3. What a rare flower it is!

4. That flower smells wonderful!

5. Those flowers are amazingly tiny!

6. Please place the tree here.

Directions: Unscramble the words to make a sentence. Write each sentence. Use periods and exclamation marks correctly.

7. flowers away please put the

_____

8. is so beautiful this garden

_____

Notes for Home: Your child identified and wrote imperative and exclamatory sentences. *Home Activity:* Together, write a short story about an exciting adventure. Make sure your child writes at least two imperative sentences and two exclamatory sentences.

© Scott Foresman 4

Imperative and Exclamatory Sentences

Directions: Look at the sentence in each space. Underline each imperative sentence. Shade each space with an exclamatory sentence.

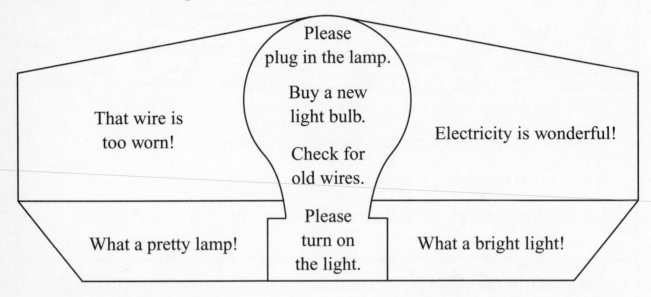

That wire is too worn!

Please plug in the lamp.

Buy a new light bulb.

Check for old wires.

Electricity is wonderful!

What a pretty lamp!

Please turn on the light.

What a bright light!

Directions: Decide if each sentence below is imperative or exclamatory. Write a period or an exclamation mark on the line. Then write **imperative** or **exclamatory.**

1. Pick up the lamp _____   _____

2. It was so expensive _____   _____

3. That old lamp still works great _____   _____

4. Please change the bulb _____   _____

5. What an unusual lamp shade _____   _____

6. Turn on the light _____   _____

Write Safety Rules

On a separate sheet of paper, write imperative and exclamatory sentences about how to use electricity safely.

Notes for Home: Your child identified imperative and exclamatory sentences. *Home Activity:* Have your child create a collage of imperative and exclamatory sentences, using words cut out from magazines. Have your child label them as *imperative* or *exclamatory.*

Simple Sentences

Directions: Read each group of words. Write **S** if it is a sentence.
Write **NS** if it is not a sentence. For each sentence, underline the simple subject once and the simple predicate twice.

_____ 1. Matthew will go to a new school in September.

_____ 2. He has worried about it all summer.

_____ 3. Meeting new teachers and students.

_____ 4. This smart boy made some plans.

_____ 5. Memorized a map of the school.

Directions: Think of a time you have been afraid of something. Write five sentences about that time. Underline each simple subject once and each simple predicate twice.

6. _____

_____

7. _____

_____

8. _____

_____

9. _____

_____

10. _____

_____

© Scott Foresman 4

Notes for Home: Your child identified the subjects and predicates in simple sentences and wrote sentences. *Home Activity:* Look at comics in a newspaper. Have your child tell which statements the characters are saying are sentences that contain a subject and a predicate.

Name _____

Compound and Complex Sentences

A **simple sentence** expresses one complete thought. A **compound sentence** contains two simple sentences joined by a comma and a connecting word such as *and, but,* or *or.*

> **Simple sentences:** My mother went out. I was home alone.
> **Compound sentence:** My mother went out, and I was home alone.

A **complex sentence** contains a simple sentence combined with a group of words that cannot stand on its own.

> **Complex sentence:** When my mother left, I was home alone.
>   group of words   simple sentence

Directions: Write whether each sentence is **compound** or **complex**.

_____ **1.** When I turned the corner, I heard a strange noise.

_____ **2.** The noise grew louder, and I was scared.

_____ **3.** Before I knew it, I was running.

_____ **4.** I saw a police car, and I told the officer what I had heard.

_____ **5.** When we saw the garbage truck, we both laughed.

Directions: Write **Yes** if the underlined words can stand alone to make a sentence. Write **No** if they cannot stand alone.

_____ **6.** <u>You are alone</u>, but you wish you weren't.

_____ **7.** <u>Because you are scared</u>, you run fast.

_____ **8.** You fall, or <u>you are knocked down</u>.

_____ **9.** <u>When your face is licked</u>, you start to laugh.

_____ **10.** You hug your dog, and <u>you give him a treat</u>.

Notes for Home: Your child identified compound and complex sentences. *Home Activity:* Read a newspaper article. Challenge your child to find compound and complex sentences in it.

Compound and Complex Sentences

Directions: Make a compound sentence by joining the simple sentences with a comma and one of these words: *and, but,* or *or.*

1. We watched a TV movie. We didn't see the end.

_____

2. Something went wrong with the set. The picture disappeared.

_____

3. The screen went dark. The sound stopped too.

_____

4. My dad would fix the set. We would replace it.

_____

5. My brother turned the radio on. We listened to the news.

_____

Directions: Write **Yes** if the underlined words can stand alone to make a sentence. Write **No** if they cannot stand alone.

_____ 6. <u>Because my parents were at Open School Night,</u> I was home alone.

_____ 7. I was reading, and <u>the lights went out.</u>

_____ 8. Was it just my house, or <u>was it a neighborhood blackout?</u>

_____ 9. <u>When I looked outside,</u> the whole neighborhood was dark.

_____ 10. Since all the electric power was off, <u>I used my flashlight.</u>

Write a Paragraph

Think of a problem you solved. On a separate sheet of paper, write a paragraph that tells how you solved it. Include compound and complex sentences.

Notes for Home: Your child identified compound and complex sentences. *Home Activity:* Point to two objects in the room. Ask your child to make up a compound sentence (contains two simple sentences and a connecting word) that compares the objects.

© Scott Foresman 4

Compound and Complex Sentences

RETEACHING

Read the compound sentence. It is made of two simple sentences. Circle the word **and** in the sentence.

   1. The pitcher throws the ball, and the batter hits it.

Read the complex sentence. It is made up of a simple sentence and a group of words that cannot stand alone as a sentence.

   2. When I threw it as hard as I could, the ball sailed away.

A **simple sentence** expresses one complete thought. It has one subject and one predicate. A **compound sentence** contains two simple sentences joined by the word **and.** A **complex sentence** contains a simple sentence and another group of words that cannot stand alone as a complete sentence.

Directions: Read each sentence. Then circle **compound** or **complex**.

   1. The catcher crouches behind the plate, and the
   pitcher throws the first ball.   compound   complex

   2. When the ball comes, the batter hits it solidly.   compound   complex

   3. The shortstop runs toward the ball because that
   is his job.   compound   complex

   4. The ball hops past the shortstop, and the batter
   runs to first base.   compound   complex

Directions: Complete each compound or complex sentence.

   5. When the game begins, _____

   6. A batter hits a high ball, and _____

   7. The home team wins, and _____

Notes for Home: Your child identified compound and complex sentences. *Home Activity:* Have your child combine pairs of sentences to form compound sentences. Then write pairs of word groups for your child to combine to create complex sentences.

Compound and Complex Sentences

Directions: Write **compound** or **complex** for each sentence.

1. Mozart was young, and he was famous. _____

2. When he was three, he played music. _____

3. Mozart read music, and he wrote it too. _____

4. He wrote melodies for many instruments because he enjoyed it. _____

5. He went on tours, and crowds cheered him. _____

6. If you say "The Magic Flute," someone might think of Mozart. _____

7. Because of Mozart, more people were interested in the piano. _____

8. It was new, and few people played it. _____

Directions: Add a simple sentence or a group of words. Write each compound or complex sentence.

9. Music makes me smile, because _____ .

   _____

10. I like to sing, and _____ .

   _____

11. We can listen, and _____ .

   _____

Write a Story

On a separate sheet of paper, write a story about a musician you like. Use compound and complex sentences Begin with a compound sentence that starts:

   I have a favorite musician, and _____ .

Notes for Home: Your child identified and wrote compound and complex sentences. *Home Activity:* Read your child's story about a favorite musician. Have him or her point out to you which sentences are compound and which are complex.

Subjects

Directions: Underline the complete subject in each sentence. Then circle each simple subject. (There may be more than one in a sentence.)

1. My cousin visited New York City last week.

2. The busy, noisy streets frightened Andrew.

3. The traffic moved too fast.

4. Andrew and his brother preferred to see New York from their hotel window.

5. Andrew became braver after a few days, however.

Directions: Add a complete subject to each group of words to make your own sentence. Write your sentence on the line. Then circle the simple subject.

6. can be a good place to live

_____

7. would be a wonderful place to visit

_____

8. can usually be found in a big city

_____

9. might be hard to find in the city

_____

10. might not be very happy in a city

_____

Notes for Home: Your child identified and used subjects in sentences. *Home Activity:* Have your child identify the subjects of some sentences in a favorite book or magazine. Suggest that your child create new sentences using the same subjects.

Name_____

from **The Cricket in Times Square**

Nouns

A **noun** is a word that names one or more persons, places, or things.

Persons: Many <u>actors</u> and <u>musicians</u> live in the city.
Places: Many actors live in the <u>city</u> and the <u>suburbs</u>.
Things: Tall <u>buildings</u> are part of a city's <u>skyline</u>.

Directions: One noun in each sentence is underlined. Circle the other noun or nouns.

1. I grew up in the <u>city</u>, near the river.

2. We lived on the first floor of a tall <u>building</u>.

3. Cars and <u>buses</u> rolled past my window.

4. A doctor and a plumber lived in two <u>apartments</u> down the hall.

5. My family went to see a <u>house</u> in the country.

6. I didn't want to move, but my parents and my <u>brother</u> did.

7. We left the <u>city</u> and drove in a big van.

8. I had never smelled such clean <u>air</u> or seen so many cows.

9. I thought my <u>parents</u> had decided to become farmers.

10. Then I heard them talking on the <u>phone</u> about their new store.

Directions: One of the underlined words in each sentence is a noun. Circle that noun.

11. I <u>suppose</u> I could get used to open <u>spaces</u>.

12. One problem is that it's hard to <u>meet</u> other <u>people</u>.

13. You can't <u>just</u> wait by your <u>door</u>.

14. I don't want my <u>best</u> friend to be a <u>cow</u>!

15. <u>Where</u> will I find new human <u>friends</u>?

© Scott Foresman 4

Notes for Home: Your child identified nouns. *Home Activity:* Have your child look around the house and write names and other nouns for as many people, places, and things as possible.

Nouns 27

Nouns

Directions: Circle all the nouns in the following sentences.

1. I grew up in the country, surrounded by farms and woods.

2. The closest village was five miles away.

3. Every single day I saw the same buildings, animals, and trees.

4. Then a letter came from my cousin.

5. He begged me to visit him at his house.

6. I couldn't make up my mind, because I had never been in the city.

7. It sounded like a rough, tough place.

8. What if I didn't get another chance?

9. I packed my best clothes, my toothbrush, and my umbrella.

10. I left under a bright, sunny sky.

Directions: Add a noun that makes sense to complete each sentence. Write the noun on the line to the left.

_____ 11. A car splashed through a _____, drenching me.

_____ 12. That was not a good _____ to begin my visit!

_____ 13. In my cousin's big house, I slept on a very soft _____.

_____ 14. Still, there wasn't a single _____ for a country cat to eat.

_____ 15. I was happy to scamper back to my _____.

Write a Tale

On a separate sheet of paper, write your own tale about going somewhere new and strange. Use nouns to describe who and what you see.

Notes for Home: Your child found nouns in some sentences and supplied nouns in others. *Home Activity:* Take a walk or a ride around your neighborhood. Have your child make a list of as many nouns as possible. Nouns may include places, names on signs, products in stores, and so forth.

Name _____

from **The Cricket in Times Square**

Nouns

RETEACHING

The nouns are underlined. Write one noun to answer each question.

1. Are you a <u>boy</u> or a <u>girl</u>? _____ (person)

2. Do you like a <u>town</u> or a <u>city</u> better? _____ (place)

3. Do you write with a <u>pen</u> or a <u>pencil</u>? _____ (thing)

A **noun** names a person, place, or thing. It gives information.

Directions: Write the three nouns in each sentence.

1. The girl threw the ball to the boy.

   _____

2. Many students play sports at school.

   _____

3. That girl kicked the ball over the tree.

   _____

4. Lin was a player on our team.

   _____

5. The teacher took the class to the playground.

   _____

Directions: Circle the nouns in each sentence.

6. Some athletes wear uniforms.

7. Many swimmers have red suits.

8. Sue belonged to a good team.

9. The crowd cheered the divers.

10. A student on the bench was tired.

Property of
Raugust Library
6070 College Lane
Jamestown, ND 58405

 Notes for Home: Your child identified nouns in sentences. ***Home Activity:*** Together, think of two categories. (For example: *sports; foods*) Have your child list as many nouns as possible that fit in each category.

© Scott Foresman 4

Nouns 29

Nouns

Directions: On the lines below, write the three nouns that are in each sentence.

1. Chicago is a city with many fine museums.

2. Those paintings on the wall have bright colors.

3. Some of the artists drew with pencils on paper.

4. The sketches hang in frames around the room.

5. The statue in the hall is made of marble.

1. _____   _____   _____

2. _____   _____   _____

3. _____   _____   _____

4. _____   _____   _____

5. _____   _____   _____

Directions: Change one noun in each sentence. Write the new sentence.

6. Jorge drew a picture of the fruit.

_____

7. The colors in the painting catch my eye.

_____

8. The artist used strong lines in this drawing.

_____

9. The photograph shows the view from the window.

_____

Write a Poem

Write a poem about a painting or a statue you have seen. Write on a separate sheet of paper. Use nouns in your sentences.

Notes for Home: Your child identified and wrote nouns in sentences. *Home Activity:* Have your child write sentences describing a room in your home. Make sure he or she uses at least two nouns in each sentence.

Name _____

Nouns

Directions: Circle all the nouns in the following sentences.

1. My family lives on the fifteenth floor of a building in the city.

2. Visitors to our apartment take the elevator to the top.

3. Although our dad loves the city, he misses his garden.

4. My father appeared one day with huge bags, tiny plants, shovels, and other tools.

5. That amazing man had decided to grow vegetables on the roof!

6. My mother and sister helped him carry the things up the stairs.

7. Our farmer poured dirt from the bags into big pots and set the plants in the soil.

8. The days were hot and sunny, and we kept pouring water on our little farm.

9. When the summer ended, we invited friends for a dinner of beans, tomatoes, and broccoli.

10. Our family and guests finished our whole crop in just one meal!

Directions: Fill in each blank with a noun that makes sense in the sentence. Write each noun on the line to the left.

_____ 11. If I had a garden, I would grow _____.

_____ 12. A garden needs lots of _____, if the plants are to grow.

_____ 13. A _____ is a tool that gardeners are likely to use often.

_____ 14. City people usually get their food from _____.

_____ 15. Some people, however, grow their own _____, even in the city.

Notes for Home: Your child identified nouns. *Home Activity:* Read a story to your child. Then go back and ask your child to pick out words that name people, places, and things.

© Scott Foresman 4

Proper Nouns

A **proper noun** names a particular person, place, or thing. The words *Carmen, Florida,* and *April* are proper nouns. Begin proper nouns with capital letters. Nouns that are not proper nouns are called **common nouns.** The words *girl, state,* and *month* are common nouns.

Common nouns: We walked down the <u>street</u>.
At the <u>corner</u>, an <u>officer</u> was directing <u>traffic</u>.

Proper nouns: We walked down <u>Third</u> <u>Street</u>.
At the corner, <u>Officer Ortiz</u> was directing traffic.

Directions: Read the following paragraph. Each underlined noun has a number next to it. Write **C** if the underlined noun is a common noun. Write **P** if the underlined noun is a proper noun. Rewrite the proper nouns correctly

Do you love **1.** <u>nature</u> but live in a **2.** <u>city</u>? If you look carefully, you'll see plenty of natural **3.** <u>life</u>. You don't need to go to **4.** <u>yellowstone national park</u> or the **5.** <u>florida everglades</u>. You don't need a large outdoor place like **6.** <u>central park</u> in **7.** <u>new york city</u>. On your own **8.** <u>block</u> there may be a **9.** <u>crack</u> in the **10.** <u>sidewalk</u>. Start there.

1. _____   6. _____

2. _____   7. _____

3. _____   8. _____

4. _____   9. _____

5. _____   10. _____

Notes for Home: Your child identified common and proper nouns and used capital letters to write proper nouns. ***Home Activity:*** Ask your child to use common nouns to identify persons, places, and things in your home. Then ask your child to replace each noun with a proper noun.

Proper Nouns

Directions: Write a proper noun to replace the underlined words in the following sentences.

_____ 1. One day <u>my friend</u> and I had a real adventure.

_____ 2. We were walking on <u>our street</u>.

_____ 3. We saw <u>our neighbor</u> and some other people standing around.

_____ 4. Just then, <u>a police officer</u> drove up.

_____ 5. "What's this?" he asked <u>one woman</u>, who was holding something.

_____ 6. "I was in <u>the park</u> and found this injured bird," she answered.

_____ 7. "I can't bring a bird all the way to <u>the animal hospital</u>," she continued.

_____ 8. "No, but <u>a veterinarian</u> has a clinic around the corner," I said.

_____ 9. "I have to be at <u>a downtown building</u> in ten minutes," the woman said. "Could someone else take the bird to the clinic?"

_____ 10. "We'll go," I told her. "Great!" said <u>a man</u> who had been listening to us.

Write a News Story

On a separate sheet of paper, write a news story about an interesting event that happened near where you live. Think about these reporter questions as you write: Who? What? When? Where? Why? and How? Use as many proper nouns as possible.

Notes for Home: Your child substituted proper nouns for common nouns. *Home Activity:* Encourage your child to tell you about the day's events, substituting proper nouns *(Jefferson Elementary School)* for common nouns *(school)*.

Name _____

Proper Nouns

Match the nouns. Draw a line from a common noun to the proper noun that matches it.

Common Noun	**Proper Noun**
1. man	Kennedy Parkway
2. country	George Washington
3. road	United States

A **common noun** names any of a kind or group of persons, places, or things. A **proper noun** names a particular person, place, or thing. Each important word in a proper noun begins with a capital letter.

Directions: Write each underlined noun in the correct column.

<u>Laura Salerno</u> visited her <u>cousins</u> in <u>Brooklyn</u>. The whole <u>family</u> rode a <u>boat</u> around <u>Manhattan</u>. They met some <u>Italians</u> there. Laura liked her <u>trip</u>.

Common Nouns	**Proper Nouns**
1. _____	5. _____
2. _____	6. _____
3. _____	7. _____
4. _____	8. _____

Directions: Circle the proper noun or proper nouns in each sentence.

9. The Statue of Liberty has many visitors.

10. The statue is on Liberty Island in New York Harbor.

11. France gave this gift to the United States.

12. People can climb it for a view of New York.

Notes for Home: Your child identified proper nouns. *Home Activity:* List familiar places or people. *(park, store, neighbor, friend)* Have your child write a proper noun for each noun you wrote. *(Lee Park, Northbrook Foods, Mrs. Washbein, Lizzie Webster)*

© Scott Foresman 4

Proper Nouns

Directions: Write a proper noun for each common noun. Use capital letters.

1. a state   _____   **5.** a river   _____

2. a neighbor   _____   **6.** a dog   _____

3. a day   _____   **7.** a date   _____

4. a doctor   _____   **8.** a city   _____

Directions: Write each sentence. Replace the underlined noun with a proper noun.

9. Jack sails on <u>a lake</u> in Ohio.

_____

10. Jack also fishes in <u>a lake</u>.

_____

11. <u>A man</u> sails with Jack on weekends.

_____

12. Jack wants to sail on <u>an ocean</u> someday.

_____

13. Mrs. Wright will sail there on <u>a holiday</u>.

_____

Write a List of Proper Nouns

On a separate sheet of paper, write a list of proper nouns. Write the names of a river, a president, a date, a doctor, a park, and a country.

Notes for Home: Your child identified and wrote proper nouns in sentences. *Home Activity:* Have your child write a description of your neighborhood, using at least five proper nouns.

Name _____

Common and Proper Nouns

Directions: Read the nouns in the box. Write each noun in the correct
column. Remember to write proper nouns with capital letters.

kangaroo	circus
debby's pet store	dr. ruiz
new england dog show	veterinarian
elephant	harold
puppy	reed animal hospital

Common Nouns

1. _____
2. _____
3. _____
4. _____
5. _____

Proper Nouns

6. _____
7. _____
8. _____
9. _____
10. _____

Directions: Replace the underlined words in each sentence with a proper noun.
Write each proper noun on the line.

_____ 11. I was surprised when <u>our neighbor</u> got a new pet.

_____ 12. I was even more surprised when <u>the pet</u> turned out to
be a little duckling.

_____ 13. Our neighbor got the duckling from the <u>animal
shelter</u>.

_____ 14. Someone had found it quacking and alone near <u>the
town lake</u>.

_____ 15. The duckling loved to visit people and soon learned
to fly across <u>the street</u> to avoid cars.

© Scott Foresman 4

Notes for Home: Your child identified and wrote common and proper nouns. *Home Activity:*
Encourage your child to name people, animals, and places you know, using common nouns
first and then proper nouns.

Regular Plural Nouns

Nouns that name one person, place, or thing are **singular nouns. Plural nouns** name more than one person, place, or thing.

- Add **-s** to form the plural of most nouns.

    monkey/monkeys   pig/pigs   cat/cats   snake/snakes

- Add **-es** to form the plural of nouns that end in **ch, sh, s, ss,** or **x.**

    bunch/bunches   wish/wishes   gas/gases   fox/foxes   glass/glasses

- To form the plural of nouns that end in a **consonant** and a **y,** change the **y** to **i** and add **-es.**

    penny/pennies   baby/babies   party/parties   lady/ladies

Directions: Write the plural form of each underlined noun on the line.

_____ **1.** My <u>friend</u> says that I live in a zoo.

_____ **2.** It all started with a stray <u>dog</u>.

_____ **3.** Soon after she came to live with us, she had a <u>puppy</u>.

_____ **4.** Yes, that means getting another animal <u>dish</u>.

_____ **5.** Then my friend Mel was moving to Mexico, so she gave me her <u>hamster</u>.

_____ **6.** Next, my little brother wanted a <u>lizard</u>.

_____ **7.** My sister brought home a <u>tadpole</u> from the lake.

_____ **8.** Before long, it turned into a <u>frog</u>.

_____ **9.** My older brother decided to raise a racing <u>pigeon</u>.

_____ **10.** "What's next?" my friend asked me. "A <u>pony</u>?"

Notes for Home: Your child added *-s* or *-es* to nouns to show more than one person, place, or thing. **Home Activity:** Take a walk through your house. Have your child name the things he or she sees using singular and plural nouns *(one sofa, two chairs)*.

Regular Plural Nouns

Directions: Write **P** if the noun is plural. Write **S** if the noun is singular. Then, write the plural form of each singular noun.

1. rabbits _____   6. stripes _____

2. pellet _____   7. monkey _____

3. tails _____   8. circus _____

4. family _____   9. snake _____

5. kitten _____   10. tanks _____

Directions: Write the plural forms of the nouns in each sentence.

_____ **11.** A ferret can be a great pet.

_____ **12.** My ferret likes to play with a ball and a bell.

_____ **13.** It likes to sleep in a special bed and on the floor of its tank.

_____ **14.** Unlike a rat, a ferret is not a rodent.

_____ **15.** Having a ferret is not as strange as having a skunk or an ocelot.

Write About a Pet

On a separate sheet of paper, write about a pet you have or would like to have. Describe where it lives, what it eats, and what things it likes to play with. Circle all the regular plural nouns.

Name _____

Regular Plural Nouns

Read the chart. Circle the **-s** or **-es** ending in each plural noun.

add **-s**	days cups boys paths seas
add **-es**	riches dishes dresses boxes buses

A **singular noun** names one person, place, or thing. A **plural noun** names more than one person, place, or thing. Add **-s** or **-es** to spell the plural forms of most nouns.

Directions: Complete the chart. Write each noun in the correct column.

axes   cobra   desert   goats
brushes   colts   eagles   house
banana   couches   ferns   peaches

Singular Nouns   **Plural Nouns**

1. _____   5. _____   9. _____

2. _____   6. _____   10. _____

3. _____   7. _____   11. _____

4. _____   8. _____   12. _____

Directions: Write the plural of each noun in ( ).

13. Those (store) sell (pet). _____

14. The (dog) saw the (bone). _____

15. Some (boy) sat on the (box). _____

16. (Student) rode the (bus). _____

Notes for Home: Your child identified regular plural nouns. *Home Activity:* Name objects in your home. Have your child write the plural forms of the names of the objects.

© Scott Foresman 4

Plural Nouns

Directions: Replace each underlined singular noun with a plural noun. Write the plural noun on the line.

1. The <u>student</u> saw a movie in the morning.

_____

2. The girl liked the <u>actor</u> in the movie.

_____

3. The class rode the <u>bus</u> to the movie.

_____

4. The <u>movie</u> held my attention.

_____

5. Judy made <u>lunch</u> for the group.

_____

Directions: Complete each sentence with a plural noun.

6. The actors studied their _____ for the play.

7. The performers gave two _____ each day.

8. Even _____ attended the show at school.

9. Some friends sent _____ to the actors.

10. Some people sat on _____ .

11. The actor said his _____ to the audience.

Write a Review

Write a review of a play or movie you enjoyed. Use plural nouns. Write on a separate sheet of paper.

Notes for Home: Your child wrote plural nouns in sentences. **Home Activity:** Have your child choose nouns from a page of a favorite story. Then have him or her write sentences, using plural forms of those nouns.

© Scott Foresman 4

Singular and Plural Nouns

Directions: Write **S** for nouns that are singular. After the **S,** write the plural form of the noun. Write **P** for nouns that are plural.

1. mess _____

2. penny _____

3. movies _____

4. crash _____

5. unicorn _____

6. glass _____

7. boxes _____

8. desks _____

9. treasures _____

10. hole _____

11. tray _____

12. hearts _____

13. turkey _____

14. lady _____

Directions: Write the plural form of each underlined noun on the line.

_____ 15. Ronald was on a trip with his <u>class</u>.

_____ 16. The group was crossing the river in a <u>ferry</u>.

_____ 17. Ronald wanted to buy a drink, but he had only a <u>quarter</u>.

_____ 18. He noticed some money a man had dropped under a <u>bench</u> nearby.

_____ 19. He picked up the money, thought for a <u>minute</u>, and went to look for the man.

_____ 20. The man thanked Ronald and gave him some change to buy a <u>drink</u>.

Notes for Home: Your child identified singular and plural nouns and wrote the plural form for singular nouns. **Home Activity:** Have your child identify singular nouns in a book or a magazine and write the plural form for each noun.

Name _____

Irregular Plural Nouns

Some plural forms of nouns do not end in **-s** or **-es.** To form these **irregular plurals,** you may have to change the spelling of the word.

Singular/Plural	
child/children	mouse/mice
foot/feet	ox/oxen
goose/geese	tooth/teeth
leaf/leaves	wolf/wolves
man/men	woman/women

A few nouns have the same form for both singular and plural.

deer	moose	sheep

Directions: Circle the correct plural noun in ( ) to complete each sentence.

1. Jenny wanted to go swimming with the other (childs/children).

2. First, she had to help the (women/womans) with chores on the farm.

3. The (sheeps/sheep) had to be brought in from the field.

4. The (oxen/oxes) had to be fed.

5. The (gooses/geese) needed more water.

6. There were (leafs/leaves) to be raked.

7. The dogs were let out to keep watch for (wolves/wolfs).

8. Jenny helped her aunt set traps for the (mouse/mice).

9. Finally, she ran to the water and jumped in with both (feet/foots).

10. Jenny startled a few (fish/fishs) with her splash.

© Scott Foresman 4

Notes for Home: Your child identified irregular plural nouns that do not end in -s or -es, such as *children.* **Home Activity:** Take turns naming irregular plural nouns. Use these words to tell a story about a country adventure.

Irregular Plural Nouns

Directions: Circle the correct plural noun in ( ) to complete each sentence.

1. Of all the (childs/children) at Olive Tree High School, Tanya was the most adventurous.

2. Every winter, she was first on the pond, her skates gleaming on her (foots/feet).

3. One day, Tanya looked up from skating and saw two big (moose/mooses).

4. She was so scared, her (teeths/teeth) started to chatter.

5. She thought, "I'm not afraid of (meece/mice), but I feel scared now!"

Directions: Write the plural form of each noun in ( ) to complete each sentence. Be careful. Don't let the rhymes fool you!

_____ 6. What would happen if foxes were friends with (ox)?

_____ 7. If (goose) travel on trains, do they ride in the cabooses?

_____ 8. Those three (wolf) like to loaf.

_____ 9. The (man) were cooking flapjacks in big pans.

_____ 10. These boots are too small for my (foot).

Write an Adventure Story

On a separate sheet of paper, write a short adventure story that involves different animals. It can be a funny story, if you wish. Use at least five irregular plural nouns.

 Notes for Home: Your child identified and wrote irregular plural nouns, such as *mice*. **Home** *Activity:* Make up rhymes that use irregular plural nouns such as those listed above.

Irregular Plural Nouns

Read the chart. Underline each singular noun. Circle each plural noun.

Singular Nouns		Plural Nouns
1. loaf	(the spelling changes)	loaves
2. mouse	(the spelling changes)	mice
3. sheep	(the spelling does not change)	sheep

Some plural nouns are formed in special ways. They are called **irregular plural nouns.** Pay attention to the spelling of irregular plural nouns.

Directions: Write the plural form of each noun.

1. man _____

2. wolf _____

3. life _____

4. person _____

5. leaf _____

6. deer _____

7. moose _____

8. shelf _____

Directions: Circle each plural noun that is not formed correctly. There is one in each sentence. Then write that plural noun correctly.

9. Grandma makes us scarfs. _____

10. She makes up stories about deers. _____

11. She reads about kinds of fishs. _____

12. She tells tales of ancient womans. _____

13. She also tells stories about gooses. _____

14. Some tales are about childrens. _____

15. Their foots take them far. _____

Notes for Home: Your child wrote irregular plural nouns correctly. **_Home Activity:_** Write irregular nouns, such as *thief* or *deer*, and have your child write the plural forms of the nouns.

Name _____

Irregular Plural Nouns

Directions: Write the plural form of each noun.

1. moose _____
2. tooth _____
3. calf _____
4. hoof _____
5. self _____
6. sheep _____
7. deer _____
8. woman _____

9. wife _____
10. ox _____
11. wolf _____
12. goose _____
13. man _____
14. foot _____
15. mouse _____
16. child _____

Directions: Write the plural form of each word on the line. Then choose two nouns from the list and use their plural forms in two sentences. Use one in each sentence.

child   deer   mouse   wolf

17. He saw two tiny _____ in the bushes.

18. The _____ ate three bowls of fruit.

19. Several swift _____ ran by the house.

20. Two gray _____ howled at the moon.

21. _____

22. _____

Write a Silly Story

Write a silly story about what happened when two mice explored a library. Use plural nouns. Write on a separate sheet of paper.

Notes for Home: Your child wrote irregular plural nouns. *Home Activity:* Have your child circle irregular plural nouns in a newspaper or magazine article. Then challenge him or her to use three of the irregular plural nouns in sentences.

Irregular Plural Nouns

Directions: Read each singular noun. Then circle the correct plural form for each one.

Singular	**Plural**
1. deer	deer / deers
2. wolf	wolfs / wolves
3. foot	feet / foots
4. tooth	tooths / teeth
5. woman	women / womans
6. ox	oxes / oxen
7. mouse	mices / mice
8. goose	geese / gooses
9. child	childrens / children
10. man	mans / men

Directions: Use the plural form of the noun in ( ) to complete each sentence. Write the plural noun on the line to the left.

_____ **11.** The path through the woods was covered with
_____. (leaf)

_____ **12.** One hiker put her _____ down on something hard.
(foot)

_____ **13.** Bending down to look, she picked up some large
_____. (tooth)

_____ **14.** Two other _____ suggested an explanation. (woman)

_____ **15.** They had heard _____ howling in the night. (wolf)

© Scott Foresman 4

Notes for Home: Your child chose and wrote nouns that change form in the plural, such as *children*. **Home Activity:** Encourage your child to make up a short story with the irregular plural nouns that she or he circled and wrote above.

Name _____

Possessive Nouns

A noun that shows who owns, or possesses, something is a **possessive noun.**

- Add an **apostrophe (')** and **-s** to a singular noun to make it a possessive noun.

    the **bear's** claws   the **fish's** eggs

- Add just an **apostrophe (')** to a plural noun that ends in **-s** to make it a possessive noun.

    the two **girls'** mother   these **families'** homes

- Add an **apostrophe (')** and **-s** to a plural noun that does not end in **-s** to make it a possessive noun.

    the **mice's** nest   the **men's** caps

Directions: Circle the possessive noun in ( ) to complete each sentence.

1. The (scientist's/scientists) work was hard, but she would not stop.

2. The (county's/counties) new road would go through the middle of the forest.

3. She had to find the four (bears/bears') den before the road was built.

4. Then she noticed a clue in a (tree's/trees') huge trunk.

5. She had discovered the (den's/dens') location!

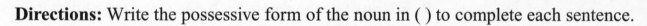

Directions: Write the possessive form of the noun in ( ) to complete each sentence.

_____ 6. The three (cubs) first days were cold and snowy.

_____ 7. The (bears) mother was sleepy, but she took good care of her babies.

_____ 8. In the spring, the (sun) rays made the cubs feel warm and frisky.

_____ 9. Once they heard bees humming and found the (bees) hive.

_____ 10. The (honey) flavor was delicious!

Notes for Home: Your child formed possessive nouns to show ownership, such as *the tree's leaves.* **Home Activity:** Ask your child to describe some favorite possessions. Then help your child make labels that use the possessive form, such as *Rosa's hat.*

Possessive Nouns

Directions: Circle the possessive noun in ( ) to complete each sentence.

1. Many (visitors/visitors') love of animals grows at Yosemite National Park.

2. A (park's/parks) wildlife includes bears, badgers, otters, and moose.

3. A (badgers/badger's) way of doing things is stubborn and fearless.

4. An (otters'/otter's) playfulness is wonderful to watch!

5. Don't you admire the (moose/moose's) huge antlers?

Directions: Write the possessive form of the noun in ( ) to complete each sentence. Then, circle **S** if the possessive noun is singular. Circle **P** if the possessive noun is plural.

S P

_____ 6. The two (hikers) trip to the forest had seemed dull.

S P

_____ 7. True, they had found three (birds) nests.

S P

_____ 8. Malcolm had even discovered some (rabbits) tracks.

S P

_____ 9. For most of the day though, the (forest) sights were fairly ordinary.

S P

_____ 10. Then Keisha saw a (grizzly) paw prints in the mud by a creek!

Write a Fantasy

Write a fantasy story about an animal family with human qualities. Use at least five possessive nouns in order to tell about the family members.

Notes for Home: Your child identified and wrote possessive nouns—nouns that show ownership, such as *the bear's claws*. **Home Activity:** Invite your child to make a list of favorite things or qualities that belong to friends and family *(my grandparents' house, Aunt Joyce's smile)*.

Possessive Nouns

Study the chart. Then complete the rules for making the possessive forms of singular and plural nouns.

Singular Noun	Singular Possessive Noun
parent / lady	parent's / lady's
man / deer	man's / deer's
Plural Noun	**Plural Possessive Noun**
parents / ladies	parents' / ladies'
men / deer	men's / deer's

1. If the noun is singular, add _____ .

2. If the plural noun ends in **-s,** add _____ .

3. If the plural noun does not end in **-s,** add _____ .

Singular and plural nouns can show ownership. To make the possessive form of a singular noun, add an **apostrophe (')** and **-s.** To make the possessive form of a plural noun that ends in **-s,** add an **apostrophe (').** To make the possessive form of a plural noun that does not end in **-s,** add an **apostrophe (')** and **-s.**

Directions: Add an apostrophe or an apostrophe and **-s** to each noun.

1. (plural) sheep _____ wool

2. mouse _____ holes

3. cat _____ meows

4. foxes _____ dens

5. trucks _____ wheels

6. driver _____ maps

7. dog _____ barks

8. (plural) elk _____ horns

9. (plural) deer _____ coats

10. birds _____ nests

11. roads _____ signs

12. whistles _____ blasts

Notes for Home: Your child identified and wrote singular and plural possessive nouns. *Home Activity:* Have your child write a story about animals and their qualities. (For example: *Once there was a giraffe with a long neck.*) Remind your child to use possessive nouns.

© Scott Foresman   4

Possessive Nouns

Directions: Use the possessive form of each noun to fill in the blanks.

children   trees   birds   gardener   flowers   park   goose

1. The _____ gates were opened for the children.

2. The children liked the _____ bright colors.

3. The _____ leaves were beginning to turn.

4. Fall flowers were the _____ favorites.

5. The _____ nests were filled with eggs.

6. The _____ trip to the park was fun.

7. The _____ honking made them laugh.

Directions: Underline the correct form of the noun in parentheses.

8. Our (gardens/garden's) flowers are beautiful.

9. Flowers can survive most (deserts/deserts') hot temperatures.

10. People admire open (prairies/prairies') bright flowers.

11. A (ponds/pond's) flowers have roots in the mud bottom.

12. The (flowers/flowers') heads are lifted to the sun.

13. (Sunflowers/Sunflowers') grow very tall.

14. (Gardeners/Gardeners') flowers are carefully tended.

Write a Song

On a separate sheet of paper, write a song about a garden. Write possessive forms of nouns in your song.

© Scott Foresman 4

 Notes for Home: Your child wrote and identified singular and plural possessive nouns in sentences. **Home Activity:** Have your child use his or her song about a garden to explain to you how to make the possessive forms of singular and plural nouns.

Predicates

Directions: Underline the complete predicate in each sentence.
Then circle each simple predicate. (There may be more than one in a
sentence.)

1. Paul Bunyan found Babe the Blue Ox during the winter of the blue snow.

2. Babe fell into a frozen river.

3. The icy water caused the ox's blue color.

4. Paul Bunyan rescued Babe and carried him back to the logging camp.

5. This famous logger built Babe a big barn.

Directions: Think about the life of a logger and his pet ox. Add a
word or words to each subject below to form a sentence. Write the
complete sentence on the line.

6. The big logger _____.

_____

7. The strong ox _____.

_____

8. The logger and his ox _____.

_____

9. The other loggers _____.

_____

10. The cook at the logging camp _____.

_____

Notes for Home: Your child identified simple and complete predicates. *Home Activity:* Play a
simple alphabet game with your child. Take turns thinking of a simple predicate, or verb, that
starts with each letter of the alphabet.

Verbs

Action verbs are words that show what action someone or something does.

The crew <u>built</u> the railroad tracks.   The train <u>raced</u> down the tracks.

Every sentence has a subject and a predicate. The main word in the subject is often a noun. The verb is the main word in the predicate.

<u>The people</u> <u>cheered at the sight of the train.</u>

Subject   Predicate

Linking verbs link, or join, the subject to a word in the predicate. The word helps tell what the subject is or what the subject is like. *Am, is, are, was,* and *were* are often used as linking verbs.

The train <u>was</u> noisy.   I <u>was</u> suprised at its size and speed.

Directions: Read the paragraph. Underline the verb in each sentence below.

1. The old train left the station. **2.** At first, it moved slowly. **3.** The engineer rang the bell. **4.** The wheels of the train rolled faster and faster. **5.** Smoke poured from the smokestack. **6.** The rumbling wheels sounded loud. **7.** The train's whistle was a warning. **8.** The train sped down the tracks. **9.** Then the old locomotive slowed its speed. **10.** It stopped at the station exactly on time.

Directions: Add a verb to complete each sentence. The verb should tell what Maria does or what Maria is like. Write the verb on the line to the left.

_____ **11.** Maria _____ out of bed early.

_____ **12.** She _____ quickly into the kitchen.

_____ **13.** Next, Maria _____ a huge breakfast.

_____ **14.** She _____ a skilled carpenter.

_____ **15.** Today, she _____ a cradle for a baby.

Notes for Home: Your child wrote action verbs and linking verbs. *Home Activity:* Play an action words game with your child. Say, for example, *Mrs. West [pause] the school bus.* Ask your child to supply the missing verb *(drives).* Switch roles and play again.

Verbs

Directions: Circle the verb in each sentence. Write **A** on the line if the verb is an action verb. Write **L** if it is a linking verb. Keep in mind that some action verbs such as *know* or *decide* show actions you cannot see.

_____ **1.** The construction crew worked very hard that hot summer day.

_____ **2.** Frederick wanted a cold drink of water and a rest.

_____ **3.** Susannah is tired and hungry.

_____ **4.** Finally, the crew finished the new road.

_____ **5.** They are proud of their smooth gray highway.

Directions: Choose a verb from the box to complete each sentence. Write the verb on the line to the left.

build	grew	felt	looks	was

_____ **6.** Didn't Lydia's family _____ their own mountain cabin?

_____ **7.** At first, they _____ nervous about doing the work themselves.

_____ **8.** After a while, they _____ more confident about their skills!

_____ **9.** Pale green paint _____ their choice for the outside walls.

_____ **10.** The finished cabin now _____ great!

Write a How-To Paragraph

On a separate sheet of paper, write a paragraph telling how to do a simple task, such as tying a small child's shoelaces. Tell the reader what to do: *First, untangle any knots in the shoelaces. Next, . . .* Use at least three verbs.

Notes for Home: Your child identified and wrote verbs—words like *build* that show action, or words like *is* that tell what the subject is or is like. ***Home Activity:*** Take turns describing a character and telling what he or she did or is like.

Verbs

Read each sentence. Complete each one with a verb from the list.

am   is   are   tame   tames

1. She _____ a clown.   2. They _____ the lion.

A **linking verb** shows being. It tells what the subject is or was. The forms of the verb **be** are often used as linking verbs. An **action verb** is a word that shows what action someone or something does.

Directions: Read each underlined verb. Circle **action verb** or **linking verb** to describe it.

1. The parade <u>was</u> colorful.   action verb   linking verb

2. Jan <u>admires</u> the costumes.   action verb   linking verb

3. The horses <u>were</u> graceful.   action verb   linking verb

4. Tiny dogs <u>danced</u> happily.   action verb   linking verb

5. I <u>am</u> a tumbler.   action verb   linking verb

6. I <u>jump</u> high into the air.   action verb   linking verb

Directions: Circle each linking verb. Underline each action verb.

7. I like the circus.

8. P. T. Barnum was the most famous circus owner.

9. His circus delighted huge crowds everywhere.

10. Circuses were small long ago.

11. A modern circus often is big.

12. Circus people are skillful performers.

13. They invent new tricks all the time.

Notes for Home: Your child identified action and linking verbs in sentences. *Home Activity:* Have your child look at a favorite book. Have him or her make a list of all the verbs on one page and say whether they are action or linking verbs.

Verbs

Directions: Write an action verb to replace the underlined linking verb in each sentence. The new verb may change the meaning of the sentence. If you need ideas, pick a verb from the box. Remember to write the form of the verb that fits the subject and tense of the sentence.

| float | shine | dance | wave | walk | play | cry |

1. The pencil <u>is</u> on the page.

   _____

2. The sun's rays <u>are</u> in the air.

   _____

3. A cloud <u>is</u> in the sky.

   _____

4. The wind <u>was</u> there all night.

   _____

5. Along the shore the waves <u>were</u>.

   _____

Directions: Imagine that one of the sentences above is the beginning of a story. Using action and linking verbs, write the next two or three sentences of the story.

_____

_____

_____

Notes for Home: Your child changed sentences by adding interesting verbs. *Home Activity:* Say simple sentences to your child. *(I walked down the street. I went there.)* Have your child replace the verbs with more interesting verbs.

Verbs

Directions: Write the verb in each sentence on the line. Remember that some verbs show what action someone or something does. Other verbs link, or join, subjects to words in predicates. A linking verb helps to tell what the subject is or what the subject is like.

_____ 1. Once a lonely pig wanted a friend very much.

_____ 2. Then one day a spider appeared in the barn.

_____ 3. The spider's name was Charlotte.

_____ 4. Soon the pig and the spider shared a wonderful friendship.

_____ 5. The pig Wilbur felt so happy.

Directions: Use each of the following words as the verb in a sentence. Write the sentence on the line.

6. laughed

_____

7. wrote

_____

8. am

_____

9. *felt* as an action verb

_____

10. *felt* as a linking verb

_____

Notes for Home: Your child identified action and linking verbs. *Home Activity:* Go back over items 3 and 5 that use linking verbs in this activity. Ask your child to circle each subject and the word in each sentence that renames or describes the subject.

Name _____

Verbs in Sentences

The subject and the verb in a sentence must work together, or **agree.** Decide whether a noun subject is singular (one) or plural (more than one). Then use the verb form that agrees with it: Jay <u>works</u>. Lumberjacks <u>work</u>.

If the verb shows action that is occurring now, or if it tells what the subject is like now, follow these rules:

- Add **-s** or **-es** to many verbs to make them agree with singular noun subjects. For verbs that end in a **consonant** and **y,** change the **y** to **i** before adding **-es.**

This hot <u>breakfast</u> <u>looks</u> good!
The <u>cook</u> <u>fries</u> more eggs.

- For the verb **be,** use *is* to agree with singular noun subjects and *are* to agree with plural noun subjects.

The <u>temperature</u> outside the cabin <u>is</u> cold.
The <u>lumberjacks</u> <u>are</u> warm from the hot food.

Directions: Circle the correct form of the verb in ( ) to complete each sentence. Write **S** if the subject is singular. Write **P** if the subject is plural.

_____ **1.** The snow (fall/falls) on the woods.

_____ **2.** Ice (freeze/freezes) on the lake.

_____ **3.** Rabbits (run/runs) across the snow.

_____ **4.** Their tracks (lead/leads) to their burrows.

_____ **5.** Meanwhile, the bears (sleep/sleeps) in their den.

_____ **6.** All winter, the woods (is/are) very quiet.

_____ **7.** A person (hear/hears) only the sound of the wind.

_____ **8.** In spring, the ice (melts/melt).

_____ **9.** Animals (wakes/wake) from their long sleep.

_____ **10.** Life (returns/return) to the woods.

Notes for Home: Your child used the correct form of verbs with singular or plural noun subjects. *Home Activity:* Offer some sentences in which the subjects need verbs ("The boy [work/works] hard"), and ask your child to choose the right verb for each sentence.

© Scott Foresman 4

Name _____

Verbs in Sentences

Directions: Circle the correct form of the verb in ( ) to complete each sentence. Write **S** if the subject is singular. Write **P** if the subject is plural. Remember that a verb must agree with its subject.

_____ 1. Logging camps (supplies/supply) wood to paper mills and furniture companies.

_____ 2. Paper mills (makes/make) paper out of wood pulp from trees.

_____ 3. That carpenter in the blue overalls (is/are) also an instructor.

_____ 4. Her helper (saw/saws) the wood carefully.

_____ 5. The customers (like/likes) their sturdy furniture.

Directions: Use the correct form of the verb in ( ) to complete each sentence. Write the verb on the line.

_____ 6. Every morning, the sun (appear) over the frozen lake.

_____ 7. Slowly, the lumberjacks (get) out of bed.

_____ 8. Marc (eat) the smallest breakfast.

_____ 9. His sister, Marcia, (eat) much more than he does!

_____ 10. These people (need) a good meal to handle the morning's work.

Write a Description

On a separate sheet of paper, write a description of people doing hard work. Use at least five verbs. Be sure your verbs agree with their subjects. Under your description, list each verb you have used, and write whether its subject is singular or plural.

© Scott Foresman 4

Notes for Home: Your child identified the forms of verbs for singular and plural subjects: *the dog barks, the dogs bark.* **Home Activity:** Name some verbs for sounds for your child *(growl, squeak, hum).* Have your child use each verb in a sentence.

Name_____

Verbs in Sentences

RETEACHING

Complete each sentence with the verb from the box that makes sense.

1. The girl _____ a flute.

2. She _____ the music pages.

3. The boys _____ the violins.

4. They _____ at concerts.

perform
holds
turns
play

Notice that when a singular noun or pronoun is the subject of a sentence, the verb is written with **-s** or **-es**. When a plural noun or plural pronoun is the subject of a sentence, the verb is written without **-s** or **-es**.

A verb in the present tense must agree with the subject of the sentence. With **he**, **she**, **it**, or a singular noun, add **-s** or **-es** to the verb.

Directions: Draw a line to connect each subject and verb that go together.

1. The flute   plays the trumpet.

2. We   sounds like a bird.

3. Jamal   take our music lessons.

Directions: Write the correct form of each verb in ( ).

4. Ms. Ames _____ (teach/teaches) music.

5. The girls _____ (dance/dances) well.

6. They _____ (practice/practices) every day.

Notes for Home: Your child used verbs that agreed with the subjects of sentences. **Home Activity:** Write three subjects, such as *the cats, our house, you and me,* and have your child write sentences, using the subjects you wrote and verbs which agree.

Verbs in Sentences 59

© Scott Foresman 4

Verbs in Sentences

Directions: Write the verb in ( ) that agrees with each subject.

1. The children _____ a song. (sing/sings)

2. Asako _____ the piano. (play/plays)

3. The director _____ the singers. (lead/leads)

4. The audience _____ the musical. (watch/watches)

5. We _____ for the children. (clap/claps)

6. The music _____ beautiful. (sound/sounds)

Directions: Write each sentence using the verb in ( ) correctly.

7. The singers (prepare) a song.   10. The students (learn) quickly.
8. The director (train) them.   11. Asako (wish) for a solo.
9. They (work) together.   12. Audiences (like) Asako.

7. _____

8. _____

9. _____

10. _____

11. _____

12. _____

Write About a Song

Use verbs in the present tense to write about a song you recently learned. Be sure
the verbs agree with the subjects. Write on a separate sheet of paper.

© Scott Foresman 4

Notes for Home: Your child wrote verbs in sentences correctly. ***Home Activity:*** Have your
child write sentences with blanks instead of verbs. Then fill in verbs. Have your child check
to make sure the verbs you wrote agree with the nouns in the sentences.

Subject-Verb Agreement

REVIEW

Directions: Circle the action verb in ( ) that agrees with the subject in each sentence. Write the verb on the line.

_____ 1. Today some people (visits/visit) a ranch during their vacations.

_____ 2. A loud bell (wakes/wake) everyone early in the morning.

_____ 3. The cook (makes/make) a hearty breakfast.

_____ 4. A ranch manager (tells/tell) the workers their chores for the day.

_____ 5. Sometimes grown-ups (helps/help) the ranch hands.

_____ 6. Occasionally they even (brands/brand) cattle.

_____ 7. Children often (rides/ride) horses out to the range.

_____ 8. At night, music (echoes/echo) across the ranch.

_____ 9. Visitors (practices/practice) square dances.

_____ 10. Soon people of all ages quickly (falls/fall) asleep.

Directions: Circle the linking verb in ( ) that agrees with the subject in each sentence. Write the verb on the line.

_____ 11. Many ranches (is/are) located in the Southwest.

_____ 12. The Double X Ranch (has/have) been in Arizona for almost 300 years.

_____ 13. Luis Martinez (was/were) the original owner.

_____ 14. His ancestors (has/have) raised cattle there ever since.

_____ 15. Martinez's great-grandson (is/are) in charge there today.

Notes for Home: Your child identified verbs that agree with their subjects. *Home Activity:* Because oral repetition helps students become familiar with the sound of correct agreement between subjects and verbs, have your child read the sentences in this activity aloud to you.

© Scott Foresman 4

Verb Tenses: Present, Past, and Future

The tense of a verb is a form that tells about time. It lets you know *when* something happens. A verb in the **present tense** shows action that is happening now. A verb in the **past tense** shows action that has already happened. A verb in the **future tense** shows action that will happen.

Present Tense: My horse <u>gallops</u> quickly.
Past Tense: My horse <u>galloped</u> quickly.
Future Tense: My horse <u>will gallop</u> quickly.

Verbs in the past tense often end in *-ed*. Verbs in the future tense include the helping verb *will*.

Directions: Write **present, past,** or **future** to tell the tense of each underlined verb.

_____ 1. The horses <u>whinnied</u>.

_____ 2. The gauchos <u>ride</u> well.

_____ 3. They <u>will tell</u> us stories later.

_____ 4. Now they <u>rope</u> calves.

_____ 5. Yesterday, I <u>roped</u> a calf by myself!

Directions: Underline the verb in each sentence. Then write **present, past,** or **future** to tell the tense of the verb.

_____ 6. On the pampas, the grass looks very green.

_____ 7. After the rain, the air will seem damp.

_____ 8. We visited one very large farm.

_____ 9. We admired the herd of cows and the big flock of sheep.

_____ 10. I love the pampas!

 Notes for Home: Your child identified verb tenses: present, past, and future. *Home Activity:* Name an enjoyable thing to do (shopping at the market) and a time for doing it (tomorrow). Ask your child to say a sentence, using the verb correctly.

© Scott Foresman 4

Verb Tenses: Present, Past, and Future

Directions: Use the correct form of the verb in ( ) to complete each sentence. Use the verb tense named in ( ). Write the verb on the line to the left.

_____   1. We _____ ostrich eggs to make a birthday cake for Julia. (need—present)

_____   2. Last year, we _____ her a beautiful huge cake. (bake—past)

_____   3. We know the ostrich _____ us through the grass. (chase—future)

_____   4. Julia _____ her cake very much. (like—future)

_____   5. Last time we threw her a party, Julia never _____ it. (expect—past)

Directions: Choose a verb from the box that best completes each sentence. On the line to the left, write the verb in the tense named in ( ).

_____   6. The gauchos _____ the cattle into a large group. (present)

_____   7. I _____ the gauchos on the ranch last summer. (past)

_____   8. My cousin _____ me how to ride. (past)

_____   9. Every night, we _____ a delicious dinner with her family. (present)

_____   10. Next summer, she and I _____ at her ranch again. (future)

| eat |
| help |
| herd |
| show |
| stay |

Write a Journal Entry

Imagine you are spending the summer on a ranch. On a separate sheet of paper, write a journal entry telling what you did today and yesterday, and what you will do tomorrow. Use different verb tenses.

Notes for Home: Your child identified verb tenses: present *(cook)*, past *(cooked)*, and future *(will cook)*. **Home Activity:** Invite your child to write the present, past, and future tense forms of such verbs as *play (play, played, will play)* and use them in a story or a rhyme.

© Scott Foresman 4

Verb Tenses: Present, Past, and Future

These sentences use the verb **bake** in three ways. Write the underlined verb in each sentence.

1. She <u>bakes</u> apples. _____ (present tense)

2. She <u>baked</u> apples. _____ (past tense)

3. She <u>will bake</u> apples. _____ (future tense)

The **tense** of a verb shows the time of the action. A verb may be written in the **present tense**, **past tense**, or **future tense**.

Directions: Write **present**, **past**, or **future** beside each verb.

1. helps _____

2. enjoyed _____

3. will roll _____

4. learns _____

5. will want _____

6. walk _____

7. roasted _____

8. will boil _____

Directions: Complete each sentence. Write the past-tense verb in ( ).

9. Dad _____ the tomatoes. (peeled/will peel)

10. Pat and I _____ the salad. (prepare/prepared)

11. Tony _____ fresh bread. (served/will serve)

12. Mom _____ the meat. (carves/carved)

13. The family _____ together. (will work/worked)

14. People _____ themselves. (helped/help)

15. Guests _____ the dinner. (enjoy/enjoyed)

Notes for Home: Your child wrote verbs in the present, past, and future tenses. **Home Activity:** Listen to a favorite song together. Have your child point out verbs in the song and tell whether they are in the present, past, or future tense.

© Scott Foresman 4

Verb Tenses: Present, Past, and Future

Directions: Underline the verb in each sentence. Then write **present**, **past**, or **future** to show the tense.

1. Serge drilled a hole in the tree.   _____

2. He pushes a peg into the hole.   _____

3. The sap will drip into a bucket.   _____

4. We will take it to the sugarhouse.   _____

5. Max pulls it on a sled.   _____

6. We boiled it for a long time.   _____

7. The water turned to steam.   _____

8. Pure maple syrup remains.   _____

9. We will pour it on pancakes.   _____

Directions: Complete each sentence. Write the past-tense form of each verb in ( ).

10. Northern Native Americans _____ maple syrup. (discover)

11. Pioneers _____ some for clothes. (trade)

12. Traders _____ the "sweet water." (like)

13. People _____ more. (want)

14. The syrup _____ sweet. (taste)

15. Children _____ it. (enjoy)

Write a Description

On a separate sheet of paper, write a description of your favorite breakfast. Use future-tense verbs in your sentences.

 Notes for Home: Your child identified and wrote verbs in the present, past, and future tenses. *Home Activity:* Have your child write about thoughts he or she had today. Remind your child to use verbs in the present, past, and future tenses.

Verb Tenses: Present, Past, and Future

Directions: Circle the verb in each sentence. Write **present, past,** or **future** on the line to name the tense of each verb.

_____ 1. Forecasters on TV predict an approaching tornado.

_____ 2. Sometimes tornadoes will catch people outside.

_____ 3. Last year a man saved himself.

_____ 4. He jumped into a ditch.

_____ 5. Tornado warnings save many lives.

Directions: Follow the directions below. Write each new sentence on the line.

6. Rewrite sentence 1 in the past tense.

_____

7. Rewrite sentence 2 in the present tense.

_____

8. Rewrite sentence 3 in the present tense.

_____

9. Rewrite sentence 4 in the future tense.

_____

10. Rewrite sentence 5 in the future tense.

_____

Notes for Home: Your child identified the three main tenses of a verb. *Home Activity:* Ask your child to say the following verbs in all three tenses: *talk, want, laugh, watch,* and *walk.* Have your child create sentences that use each of the three tenses of *talk.*

© Scott Foresman 4

Using Correct Verb Tenses

To form the **present tense** of most verbs, add **-s** or **-es** if a subject is a singular noun or is *he, she,* or *it:* A baby bird <u>chirps</u>. The mother <u>watches</u>.

Do not add an ending to the verb if the subject is plural: Birds <u>live</u> in nests.

To form the **past tense** of most verbs, add **-ed: raked, tasted, walked.**

For most one-syllable verbs that end in a single vowel followed by a single consonant, double the final consonant before adding **-ed: hugged.**

When a verb ends in a **consonant** and **y**, change the **y** to **i** before adding **-ed: copied.**

A verb whose past tense does not end in **-ed** is called an **irregular verb.** You will need to remember how to form the past tense of irregular verbs: **held, drew, sang.**

Directions: Circle the correct verb form in ( ) to complete each sentence. Use a dictionary if you need help with irregular verbs.

1. Every year my friends (watch/watches) *The Wizard of Oz* on TV.

2. Last weekend they (see/saw) the movie again.

3. L. Frank Baum (writes/wrote) the original book.

4. Yesterday, I (asks/asked) them about the movie.

5. Tina said her favorite part (was/were) when the tornado took Dorothy to the land of Oz.

6. In Oklahoma, where we all (live/lived), we get tornadoes too.

7. Last year, a tornado (sweeps/swept) through our town.

8. We (go/went) to the cellar and stayed there for hours.

9. At first the noise of the tornado was very loud, but then suddenly it (stopped/stops).

10. After a while, we (heard/hear) the "all clear" signal and left our shelter.

Notes for Home: Your child identified verb tenses. *Home Activity:* Use four or five sentences to tell your child a story. Use the present tense (*A baby robin falls from its nest*). Then, have your child retell it using the past-tense verbs.

Using Correct Verb Tenses

Directions: Use the correct form of the verb in ( ) to complete each sentence. Write the verb on the line to the left. Use a dictionary if you need help with irregular verbs.

_____ **1.** Usually, tornadoes (move) very swiftly.

_____ **2.** Often, the powerful wind (destroy) things in its path.

_____ **3.** Yesterday, a strange whirling cloud (appear).

_____ **4.** I was walking home when I (notice) it.

_____ **5.** I (run) to a safe place as fast as I could!

Directions: Use a verb from the box to complete each sentence. Write the verb in the correct tense on the line to the left. Use a dictionary if you need help with irregular verbs.

cry	fall	place	plant	snap

_____ **6.** Last year my favorite tree _____ in a bad storm.

_____ **7.** The strong wind _____ it in two.

_____ **8.** I was so sad that I _____ for days.

_____ **9.** An hour ago, we _____ a new tree in the yard.

_____ **10.** My father dug the hole, and I _____ the tree in it.

Write a Letter to a Friend

Were you ever caught in a bad storm? Was the experience scary? What did you do? On a separate sheet of paper, write a letter to a friend about your experience. You can describe a real experience, or you can make one up. Try to use verbs in different tenses.

Notes for Home: Your child wrote verbs in different tenses to show when something occurred. **Home Activity:** Play a verb game with your child. Take turns naming a verb and naming that verb's past tense.

Using Correct Verb Tenses

RETEACHING

Read each sentence. Write the correct form of the verb in ( ) on the line.

1. The bright sun (shine—present tense) _____ .

2. Yesterday I (cook—past tense) _____ soup.

3. Then I (dip—past tense) _____ berries in chocolate.

4. I was late for school, so I (hurry—past tense) _____ .

5. I could not read what he (write—past tense) _____ .

Add **-s** or **-es** to form the present-tense form of most verbs if the subject is singular. Add **-ed** to form the past-tense form of most verbs. When a one-syllable verb ends in a single vowel followed by a single consonant, double the final consonant before adding **-ed**. When a verb ends in a consonant and **y**, change the **y** to **i** before adding **-ed**. A verb whose past-tense form does not end in **-ed** is an irregular verb. You will need to remember the forms of these verbs.

Directions: Underline the correct verb form in ( ) to complete each sentence. Use a dictionary if you need help with irregular verbs.

1. Usually my family (likes/liked) to eat dinner together.

2. Although we were busy, we (eat/ate) together every night last week.

3. Sometimes my mom (makes/make) dinner, and sometimes my dad does.

4. Last night my dad (hurry/hurried) home to make dinner.

5. Then my mom and I (jogged/jogs) after dinner.

6. When we got home, my stepbrother (ask/asked) for help with math.

7. I was tired, but I (finish/finished) my homework by eight o'clock.

8. Then I finally (went/go) to bed!

Notes for Home: Your child identified correct verb tenses in sentences. ***Home Activity:*** Have your child point out verbs in a story and tell what tense they are. Then have him or her write new sentences, using the verbs from the story. Challenge him or her to change the tenses of the verbs.

Name_____

Using Correct Verb Tenses

Directions: Use a verb from the box to complete each sentence. Write the verb in the correct tense on the line. Use a dictionary if you need help with irregular verbs.

> bake   call   decide   dry   earn   give   hug   lick
> make   start   tell   wag   wash   worry   write

_____ (present)   **1.** My teacher _____ us a week to do an assignment.

_____ (past)   **2.** I _____ about a kite on a string.

_____ (past)   **3.** Our dog _____ his tail.

_____ (past)   **4.** I wanted to play with him, so I _____ him.

_____ (past)   **5.** He came over to me and he _____ my hand.

_____ (present)   **6.** My older sister _____ dinner on Monday nights.

_____ (past)   **7.** After dinner, Sam _____ the dishes and I _____
_____   them.

_____ (past)   **8.** He _____ that he wouldn't have time to play.

_____ (past)   **9.** I _____ him he had an hour left before his bedtime.

_____ (past)   **10.** Sam was so happy that he _____ me.

_____ (present)   **11.** Renee _____ brownies and muffins to raise money for her club.

_____ (past)   **12.** She and Shaunna _____ the club a year ago.

_____ (past)   **13.** They _____ twenty dollars in one weekend.

_____ (past)   **14.** But the club hasn't _____ what to do with the money!

Notes for Home: Your child wrote verb tenses in sentences. *Home Activity:* Make flashcards with your child. Help your child identify which verbs he or she has trouble remembering how to write in the present and past tenses. Then make flashcards for the difficult verbs.

Using Correct Verb Tenses

Directions: Use the correct form of the verb in ( ) to complete each sentence. Write the verb on the line.

_____ **1.** Special dogs have (help) blind people for many years.

_____ **2.** These seeing eye dogs have (train) at special schools.

_____ **3.** Over the years, many people have (use) German shepherds as seeing eye dogs.

_____ **4.** These dogs are always (work) hard for their owners.

_____ **5.** They have (offer) independence to many.

_____ **6.** My friend Jenna is (get) a seeing eye dog.

_____ **7.** Last month, she (pick) out a young dog she liked.

_____ **8.** It (be) a German shepherd.

_____ **9.** Jenna is (wait) for the dog to finish its training.

_____ **10.** She will (take) the dog to school every day.

Directions: Circle the correct verb form in ( ) in each sentence.

11. Some special monkeys are (gave/given) other duties.

12. They are (teached/taught) special skills.

13. Many of these monkeys have (gone/went) to the homes of deaf people.

14. These monkeys are always (drew/drawing) their owner's attention to sounds such as a doorbell.

15. Getting one of these monkeys will (make/making) a big difference in a person's life.

© Scott Foresman 4

Notes for Home: Your child practiced using the correct tenses of verbs. *Home Activity:* Have your child make up sentences using the following forms of the verb *eat: eat, am eating, ate, have eaten.*

Review of Verbs

A word that shows action is a **verb.** Use the proper verb form to agree with a singular noun subject or with *he, she,* or *it* and use the proper verb form to agree with a plural subject.

Verbs in the **present tense** show action that is happening now. Verbs in the **past tense** show action that has already happened. Verbs in the **future tense** show action that will happen in the future.

> **Present:** Our dog <u>barks</u> at strangers.
>
> **Past:** Last night the dog <u>barked</u> once.
>
> **Future:** He <u>will bark</u> when you ring the bell.

A verb in the past tense often ends with **-ed.** A verb whose past-tense form does *not* end in **-ed** is called an **irregular verb.** Since it doesn't follow a pattern, you have to remember its past-tense form.

Directions: Circle the correct form of the verb in ( ) to complete each sentence.

1. Some dogs (makes/make) noise when strangers appear.

2. Sometimes a cat's behavior (provide/provides) a warning.

3. Other animals (offers/offer) other kinds of protection for their young.

4. Geese (honks/honk) loudly at strangers.

5. An angry goose (looks/look) quite dangerous.

Directions: Use the correct form of the verb in ( ) to complete each sentence. Use the verb tense named in ( ). Write the verb on the line to the left.

_____ 6. Freckles the dog _____ on the front porch. (sit—past)

_____ 7. He _____ the house all day. (guard—future)

_____ 8. Last year, he _____ a burglar. (catch—past)

_____ 9. That burglar never _____ again! (come—past)

_____ 10. No one _____ with Freckles around. (worry—future)

Notes for Home: Your child wrote verbs for singular and plural subjects and to show present, past, and future actions. ***Home Activity:*** Name a verb. Have your child give its present-tense, past-tense, and future-tense forms.

Review of Verbs

Directions: Circle the correct form of the verb in ( ) to complete each sentence.

1. Mosquitoes (flyed/flew) freely in the summer night.

2. Then the spider (catched/caught) one in her web.

3. Spiders (protect/protects) people from harmful insects.

4. Our mosquito bites (itch/itched) all last night!

5. Right now, all of us (hope/will hope) that the spider will catch more mosquitoes!

Directions: Add a verb to complete each sentence. Write the verb in the correct tense on the line to the left.

_____ 6. Yesterday, the sheep _____ peacefully in the meadow.

_____ 7. They ate the grass that grew there and _____ the water from the stream.

_____ 8. They are safe because our dogs _____ them every day.

_____ 9. Sheepdogs _____ the sheep of a flock from wandering away.

_____ 10. The sheep _____ asleep, but now they are awake.

Write an Animal Story

Have you ever wondered what animals would say to each other if they could talk? On a separate sheet of paper, write a story about two animal friends. Use different verbs, including two irregular verbs. Be sure to use correct verb tenses. Underline your verbs.

Notes for Home: Your child circled and wrote verbs to complete each sentence. **Home Activity:** Name some "fun" action verbs, such as *smile, clap, cheer, jump, spin.* Invite your child to tell you the present-tense, past-tense, and future-tense forms of each verb.

Review of Verbs

Complete each sentence. Write the correct form of the verb **walk** on the line.

Present: He _____ to the playground.

Past: Yesterday he _____ to school.

Future: Tomorrow he _____ to Jeremy's house.

Verbs in the **present tense** show action that is happening now. Verbs in the **past tense** show action that has already happened. Verbs in the **future tense** show what will happen.

Complete each sentence. Write the correct form of the verb **eat** on the line.

Present: Lorna _____ lunch at home.

Past: Yesterday Lorna _____ lunch at school.

Future: Tomorrow she _____ lunch at her grandparents' house.

Often a verb in the past tense ends with **-ed**. A verb whose past-tense form does not end in **-ed** is called an **irregular verb.**

Directions: Use the correct form of the verb in ( ) to complete each sentence. Use the verb tense named in ( ). Write the verb on the line to the left.

_____ **1.** Celia _____ an answer to her friend. (whisper—present)

_____ **2.** I _____ my hands. (wave—past)

_____ **3.** Bruce _____ on me. (call—past)

_____ **4.** "You _____ the answer," he said. (know—future)

_____ **5.** "I _____ it is forty-two." (think—present)

_____ **6.** "You _____ smart," he said. (be—present)

Notes for Home: Your child wrote verbs for singular and plural subjects and in different tenses. *Home Activity:* Talk about what you did for fun when you were your child's age, and about what you would like to do together. Use verbs in the present, past, and future tenses.

Review of Verbs

Directions: Circle the correct form of the verb in ( ) to complete each sentence. Use a dictionary if you need help with irregular verbs.

1. Our neighbors (gives/gave) us an empty box.

2. We (decides/decided) to make a rocket ship.

3. The box (were/was) so big we couldn't fit it in the house.

4. Mom (tell/told) us to leave it in the backyard.

5. All of us (played/will play) with it next weekend.

6. We (put/puts) stickers on the outside of the ship.

7. Mike (run/ran) to his house to get markers.

8. Then he and Joe (drawn/drew) windows and a door.

9. Steve (will cut/cut) a hole in the top before we can climb inside.

10. I (am/will be) the first one to sit in the ship tomorrow.

11. John (was/is) finishing the decorations inside the ship right now.

12. We (is/are) very excited about our ship!

Directions: Write sentences, using the verbs and verb tenses in ( ).

(draw—future) 13. _____

(move—past) 14. _____

(fly—present) 15. _____

© Scott Foresman 4

Notes for Home: Your child identified and wrote verbs with singular and plural subjects and in present, past, and future tenses. **Home Activity:** Read a magazine or newspaper article with your child. Have him or her find one example each of present, past, and future-tense verb forms.

Complete Subjects

Directions: Underline the complete subject in each sentence.

1. Many folk tales use animals as characters.

2. These make-believe animals talk, cry, and act just like human beings.

3. Natural events become characters in folk tales too.

4. A good storyteller can make the forces of nature seem alive.

5. The mighty wind might decide to show off its power, for example.

6. A strong, fast stream is able to float a child to safety.

7. A soft breeze grows angry and turns into a raging windstorm.

8. A thunderstorm gets tired and dozes off as a gentle drizzle.

9. Some animals persuade a little spark to grow into a dangerous fire.

10. Anything can take on human qualities in a folk tale.

Directions: Add a complete subject to each predicate to create a sentence. Your subject should have at least three words. Write your sentence on the line.

11. became angry and roared down from the mountain

_____

12. warmed all the people sitting around it

_____

13. ruined the picnic for everyone

_____

14. came running out of the cabin

_____

15. appeared in the sky and frightened us

_____

Notes for Home: Your child identified and used complete subjects in sentences. *Home Activity:* Collect four or five things from around the house. Ask your child to write a sentence about each item and underline the complete subject.

Adjectives

A word that describes a person, place, or thing is called an **adjective.** An adjective often comes before a noun, but it also can follow a noun or pronoun.

- Some adjectives tell what kind. They describe color, shape, size, sound, taste, touch, or smell: The <u>little</u> donkey trotted under its load of hay.

- Some adjectives tell how many: Are <u>two</u> men needed for the job?

- Some adjectives tell which one: Walk toward <u>that</u> restaurant.

Directions: Write the adjective or adjectives that tell more about each underlined noun.

_____ 1. The <u>wind</u> and the <u>sun</u> felt irritable.

_____ 2. They had a short <u>argument</u>.

_____ 3. This <u>quarrel</u> was about who had more strength.

_____ 4. A strong, cold <u>wind</u> blew across the field.

_____ 5. The bright, hot <u>sun</u> beat down on the land.

_____ 6. Each fierce <u>competitor</u> was determined to win.

Directions: Use the adjectives in the box to write four sentences.

cold	hot	this	bright

7. _____

8. _____

9. _____

10. _____

Notes for Home: Your child identified adjectives, words that describe persons, places, or things, in sentences. *Home Activity:* Point to objects and ask your child to describe them, using as many different adjectives as possible.

Name _____

Adjectives

Directions: Underline the adjective or adjectives in each sentence.

1. On a beautiful morning, a kind old woman decided to bake cookies.

2. She mixed ginger with the rest of the fresh ingredients and divided the sweet dough into pieces.

3. She rolled out one piece, then carefully cut it into the shape of a little man.

4. The old woman placed her special cookie in a large pan and slid it into the hot oven.

5. After a short time, the woman smelled ginger and heard a strange sound inside the oven.

6. When she opened the door, the surprised woman couldn't believe her eyes.

7. The crispy cookie-man sat up and said, "Thank you."

8. He jumped down and ran across the kitchen as fast as his little legs could go.

9. The old woman ran after him.

10. The clever cookie-man called out in a squeaky voice, "Run, run, as fast as you can. You can't catch me—I'm the cookie-man!"

Write a Folk Tale

On a separate sheet of paper, retell a folk tale or fairy tale that you know. Use at least one adjective in each sentence to describe the characters, things, and places in the story. Underline all the adjectives you use.

© Scott Foresman 4

Notes for Home: Your child identified adjectives—words that describe persons, places, or things—in sentences. **Home Activity:** Describe objects in your child's room, using only adjectives, such as *blue, fluffy, soft,* and have him or her guess what you are describing. (*a pillow*)

78 Adjectives

Name_____

Half-Chicken

Adjectives

RETEACHING

Connect the words that describe the picture.

Adjectives	Adjectives	Nouns
1. six	hard	rocks
2. some	little	turtles

Write the words you connected to complete each sentence.

3. I see _____ _____ _____ .
       (adjective)   (adjective)   (noun)

4. I see _____ _____ _____ .
       (adjective)   (adjective)   (noun)

An **adjective** describes a person, place, or thing. Adjectives can answer the questions **How many?**, **What kind?**, and **Which One?**

Directions: Tell more about each noun with two adjectives.

1. _____ _____ snails

2. _____ _____ fox

Directions: Circle the adjectives that tell **what kind, how many,** and **which one.**

3. Many leaves lay on the cold ground.

4. Two woodchucks crawled in long tunnels.

5. Ten bats stayed in dark caves.

6. One deer searched for some food.

Notes for Home: Your child identified adjectives. *Home Activity:* Have your child write a description of a perfect day. Challenge your child to use six adjectives in his or her description.

© Scott Foresman 4

Adjectives 79

Adjectives

Circle the adjectives that tell **what kind, how many,** and **which one.** Then write each adjective in the correct column.

1. Many craters are on this dusty moon.

2. Those pointy rocks are in several areas.

3. Deep valleys are in some places.

4. Twelve astronauts landed on its rough surface.

What Kind	How Many	Which One
5.	9.	13.
6.	10.	14.
7.	11.	
8.	12.	

Directions: Follow the correct path through the puzzle. Find the adjectives that tell **what kind.** Then write each one to tell more about a noun.

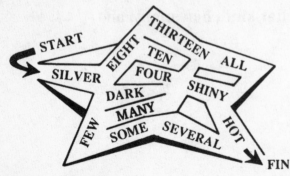

15. _____ star

16. _____ sun

17. _____ planets

18. _____ sky

Write a Poem

On a separate sheet of paper, write a poem about the night sky. Tell what you see. Use adjectives that tell what kind and how many.

Notes for Home: Your child identified adjectives that tell *what kind, how many,* and *which one.* **Home Activity:** Have your child look at a magazine article and find an example of each kind of adjective. Then have him or her use them to write new sentences.

Adjectives

Directions: Draw two lines under the articles **a, an,** and **the** in the sentences below. Then draw a circle around each adjective that tells more about the underlined noun.

1. Many <u>animals</u> were gathered for an important <u>trial</u>.

2. The noisy, crowded <u>courtroom</u> grew quiet when the judge entered.

3. Everyone admired this strong, smart <u>crow</u> in the black <u>robe</u>.

4. Chester Cow was an eager <u>witness</u>.

5. When some young <u>calves</u> waved to Chester, the judge frowned.

6. "We are here for a serious <u>trial</u>," he declared. "No waving."

7. The cows and the sheep sat on different <u>sides</u> of the courtroom.

8. The two <u>groups</u> glared at one another.

9. Who had the right to graze on the beautiful green <u>meadow</u> near the lake?

10. That important <u>question</u> would be decided here today.

Directions: Complete each sentence with an article or with an adjective that tells how many or how much. Choose a word from the box, and write it on the line to the left.

more	many	an	fifty	few

_____ 11. In the crowded courtroom sat at least _____ sheep and cows.

_____ 12. Joining them were _____ chickens, goats, pigs, and others.

_____ 13. They had waited more than _____ hour to get a seat.

_____ 14. There were very _____ animals that were not interested in today's trial.

_____ 15. The winner of the trial would have _____ grass to eat and would rule the barnyard.

 Notes for Home: Your child identified and used adjectives—words that describe persons, places, or things—in sentences. **Home Activity:** Ask your child to name five favorite people, places, and things, and then have your child write a sentence describing each one.

Using Adjectives to Improve Sentences

The sentence below does not paint a clear picture. It needs descriptive details.

Sentence: The king wanted clothes.

One way to revise it is by adding adjectives.

Adjectives Added: The <u>wealthy</u> king wanted <u>colorful</u> clothes.

Don't use more adjectives than necessary to express your ideas clearly.

Overuse of Adjectives: The wealthy, worldly, old king wanted elegant, fancy clothes.

Directions: Choose the better adjective in ( ) to complete each sentence. Write it on the line.

_____ 1. Once upon a time, two (unkind/nice) men played a cruel trick on their king.

_____ 2. Someone from the (royal/tiny) palace told them the king was tired of his suits.

_____ 3. The king wanted suits that were better than any (all/other) suits in the kingdom.

_____ 4. (These/This) two men opened a tailoring business.

_____ 5. The (eager/stingy) king ordered a new suit.

_____ 6. The tailors said they used cloth that was so unusual that (marvelous/ordinary) people couldn't see it.

_____ 7. The (vain/humble) king ordered a suit made of this cloth.

_____ 8. The (dishonest/unsuspecting) king put on his "invisible suit."

_____ 9. He paid the (greedy/golden) men with gold coins.

_____ 10. A boy on the street saw the (little/foolish) ruler and exclaimed, "His Majesty forgot to put a suit on!"

© Scott Foresman 4

Notes for Home: Your child used adjectives—words that describe nouns or pronouns—to make sentences more interesting. *Home Activity:* Have your child tell you about his or her day, using adjectives to give an interesting description.

Using Adjectives to Improve Sentences

Directions: Add an adjective to improve each sentence. Write the adjective on the line to the left.

_____ 1. "But I can explain!" insisted the _____ girl known as Goldilocks.

_____ 2. "I was sent by my _____ grandmother to the bears' house."

_____ 3. "My grandmother is the bears' _____ housekeeper."

_____ 4. "When I arrived at the _____ house, no one came to the door."

_____ 5. "I walked in the _____ door and looked around."

_____ 6. "I didn't sit in their chairs, and I didn't eat any of their _____ porridge either."

_____ 7. "I just put it in the _____ oven so it wouldn't get cold."

_____ 8. "I didn't really sleep in their _____ beds either."

_____ 9. "I was just putting on some _____ sheets."

_____ 10. "I hope you think this _____ story is interesting."

Write an Explanation

Pretend you are a character from a folk tale or fairy tale you have read, such as "Goldilocks" or "Jack and the Beanstalk." On a separate sheet of paper, write an explanation for something you did in the tale, such as wander into the three bears' cottage, or buy a hatful of beans. Use colorful adjectives to help you write vivid, interesting sentences.

Notes for Home: Your child improved sentences by adding adjectives. *Home Activity:* Play a game of "Finish the Sentence," adding adjectives to each other's sentences.

Using Adjectives to Improve Sentences

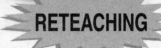

RETEACHING

The sentences below do not have descriptive details. Add an adjective to each sentence. Write it on the line.

1. The person ate _____ cake.

2. Manuel put on _____ shoes.

This sentence has too many adjectives. Draw lines through adjectives that aren't necessary.

3. My favorite, best-liked, wonderful, nice, blue sweater was in the wash.

Adding an **adjective** to a sentence is one way to add descriptive detail. Using adjectives also helps you to express your ideas more clearly.

Directions: The story below is not very descriptive or clear. Choose an adjective from the box that best fits each sentence. Write the adjective on the line. Some adjectives will not be used.

| afraid   brave   bright   colorful   dark   empty   gray   happy |
| heavy   huge   lonely   long   musty   new   old   tall |

Darron walked down the **1.** _____ sidewalk. He had never seen the street

so **2.** _____ . He was a little **3.** _____ . The streetlights were

4. _____ , but it was still hard to see clearly. When he got to the

5. _____ building, he stopped. The **6.** _____ windows looked like

rectangles. The doors were **7.** _____ . Darron closed his eyes. "I am

8. _____ ," he said. Then he went inside. The library smelled **9.** _____ .

He reached the highest shelf and took down a **10.** _____ book.

Notes for Home: Your child added adjectives to a story to make it more vivid and interesting. *Home Activity:* Read a page from a favorite story to your child, leaving out the adjectives. Have your child add adjectives of his or her choosing.

Using Adjectives to Improve Sentences

Directions: Change seven adjectives in the story to make the mood even scarier.
Use the words in the idea bank, or make up words of your own.

1.–6.

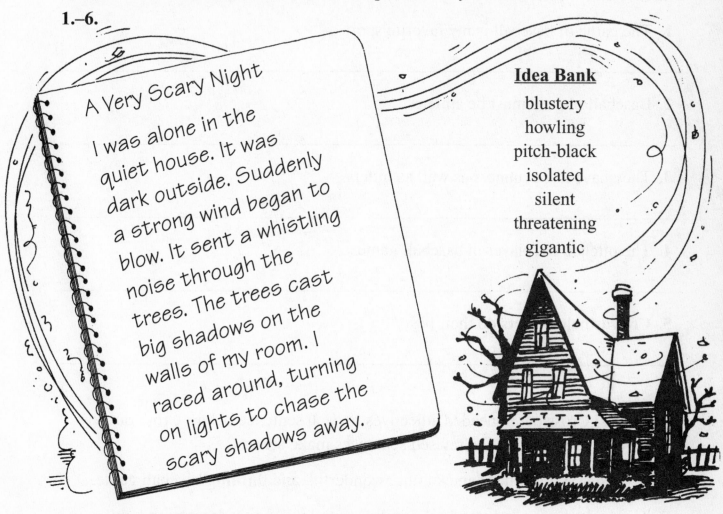

A Very Scary Night

I was alone in the quiet house. It was dark outside. Suddenly a strong wind began to blow. It sent a whistling noise through the trees. The trees cast big shadows on the walls of my room. I raced around, turning on lights to chase the scary shadows away.

Idea Bank

blustery
howling
pitch-black
isolated
silent
threatening
gigantic

Directions: Write three sentences that create a different mood of your choice.
Remember to use adjectives that help create your mood.

_____

_____

_____

Notes for Home: Your child replaced words in a story with more interesting adjectives. *Home Activity:* Have your child write a story about an exciting event. Challenge him or her to use descriptive adjectives in the story.

Name_____

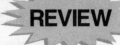

Using Adjectives to Improve Sentences

Directions: Add one or more adjectives to improve each sentence. Write your new sentence on the line. Underline your adjectives.

1. The game of baseball is my favorite sport.

_____

2. Baseball players must be athletes.

_____

3. They have to be runners as well as hitters.

_____

4. The pitcher is a player in baseball games.

_____

5. Crowds help players do their best.

_____

Directions: Cross out unneeded adjectives in each sentence below. Cross out any other words as needed so the revised sentences make sense.

6. My sister and I went to an exciting, wonderful, and thrilling baseball game.

7. The packed, crowded stands were filled with loud, noisy, screaming fans.

8. Everyone cheered for his or her best-liked and favorite team.

9. By the seventh inning, the tired and weary pitcher was becoming sloppy and weak.

10. The next batter hit a strong, soaring, terrific home run over the wall.

Notes for Home: Your child improved sentences by adding adjectives to give more detail and removing unnecessary adjectives. *Home Activity:* Have your child write sentences about something that happened today. Help your child add, take away, or replace some of the adjectives.

Name_____

Name _____

Comparative and Superlative Adjectives

Adjectives are often used to tell how people, places, and things are alike or different. In the sentence below, the **-er** ending in **newer** shows that two things are being compared.

> **Comparative:** Your bat is <u>newer</u> than mine.

The **-est** ending of **newest** in the next sentence shows that three or more things are being compared.

> **Superlative:** Carlos's bat is the <u>newest</u> of all.

Here are some patterns you can use to write comparative and superlative adjectives.
- For most adjectives that end with a consonant and **y,** change the **y** to **i** before you add **-er** or **-est: dry, drier, driest.**
- For most adjectives that end in a single consonant after a vowel, double the final consonant before adding **-er** or **-est: flat, flatter, flattest.**
- If an adjective ends with **e,** drop the final **e** before you add **-er** or **-est: safe, safer, safest.**

If you use a long adjective such as **terrific,** use **more** to compare two things. Use **most** to compare three or more. Never use **more** or **most** with the endings **-er** or **-est.**

> The other team is <u>more terrific</u> than ours.
> Carlos's team is the <u>most terrific</u> of all.

Directions: Add **-er** or **-est,** or use **more** or **most** to form comparative and superlative adjectives.

Adjective	Comparative Adjectives	Superlative Adjectives
early	1. _____	2. _____
late	3. _____	4. _____
low	5. _____	6. _____
thin	7. _____	8. _____
successful	9. _____	10. _____

Notes for Home: Your child wrote comparative and superlative forms of adjectives that compare people, places, and things. *Home Activity:* Play "Can You Top This?". Take turns. One person names an adjective, and the other person gives its comparative and superlative forms.

Comparative and Superlative Adjectives

Directions: Complete each sentence by writing the correct form of the adjective in ( ).

_____ 1. Some people think that baseball is the (exciting) sport.

_____ 2. They think it is (exciting) than football, even though it is not as rough.

_____ 3. Baseball is (slow) than basketball, but these fans still prefer it.

_____ 4. They think that going to a baseball game is the (enjoyable) way to spend an afternoon.

_____ 5. They love to watch a player who is the (strong) hitter on his team.

_____ 6. They like to argue about which runner is (fast) than another.

_____ 7. They think the players on their favorite teams are the (great) players of all.

_____ 8. If your team wins a game, it's a (happy) day than if the team loses.

_____ 9. But even if they lose, seeing the game is still (enjoyable) than staying home.

_____ 10. For the players, sportsmanship is the (important) thing of all.

Write a Description

On a separate sheet of paper, describe your favorite sport. Use comparative adjectives to compare your sport with another sport. Use superlative adjectives to compare three or more things in your description. Circle each comparative and superlative adjective you used.

© Scott Foresman 4

Notes for Home: Your child used the comparative and superlative forms of adjectives. **_Home Activity:_** Have your child tell you about an exciting day, using as many comparative and superlative adjectives as possible.

Name_____

Comparative and Superlative Adjectives

RETEACHING

Which dog won first prize in the dog show? Solve the riddle below.

bulldog

poodle

Irish setter

Riddle: The winner's tail is longer than the bulldog's tail. The winner does not have the longest tail of all. Circle the winner.

The words **longer** and **longest** are adjectives. The adjective **longer** compared two things. The adjective **longest** compared three things.

An adjective has two different forms that are useful in making comparisons. Use the **-er** form to compare two persons, places, or things. Use the **-est** form to compare three or more persons, places, or things.

Directions: Write the missing **-er** or **-est** form of each adjective.

1. clean, cleaner, _____

2. strong, _____ , strongest

3. bright, _____ , _____

Directions: Complete each sentence with an adjective that compares.

4. Bill's poodle is _____ than my dog.

5. Your collie is _____ than his collie.

6. My dog has the _____ bark of all.

Notes for Home: Your child wrote comparative and superlative adjectives. *Home Activity:* Have your child choose three characters from a book, TV show, or movie, and use comparative and superlative adjectives to compare the characters.

Comparative and Superlative Adjectives

Directions: Write the missing **-er** or **-est** form of each adjective.

1. busy   busier   _____

2. fat   _____   fattest

Directions: Use one adjective from the list to complete each sentence.

small   smaller   smallest   large   larger   largest

3. An ant is very _____.

4. A lion is _____ than a mouse.

5. A robin is _____ than an elephant.

6. The _____ animal of all is a whale.

Directions: Complete each comparison. Write the correct form of an adjective in the list. Then write a noun.

big   slow   thin   noisy   busy   large

7. Chipmunks are _____ than _____ .

8. Frogs are _____ than _____ .

9. Snails are the _____ _____ of all.

10. Worker bees are the _____ of all _____ .

Write a Story

Write a story about a pet or a wild animal you like. Describe it well by using adjectives that compare. Write on a separate sheet of paper.

Notes for Home: Your child wrote comparative and superlative adjectives in sentences. *Home Activity:* Find pictures of three animals in books or magazines. Have your child label the pictures with comparative and superlative adjectives.

© Scott Foresman 4

Name _____

Comparative and Superlative Adjectives

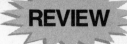

Directions: Add **-er, -est, more,** or **most** to the adjectives to form comparative and superlative adjectives.

Adjective	Comparative Adjectives	Superlative Adjectives
funny	1. _____	2. _____
pale	3. _____	4. _____
high	5. _____	6. _____
big	7. _____	8. _____
wonderful	9. _____	10. _____

Directions: Write the correct form of the adjective in ( ) to complete each sentence.

_____ **11.** Few things are (exciting) than learning about other cultures.

_____ **12.** Food is one of the (important) parts of any culture.

_____ **13.** Yesterday I went to the (large) International Fair I have ever seen.

_____ **14.** It had the (great) variety of food I have ever eaten.

_____ **15.** The Mexican tacos seemed (spicy) than usual.

_____ **16.** Indian food is often (hot) than Mexican food.

_____ **17.** The Chinese spring rolls were (delicious) than others I have eaten elsewhere.

_____ **18.** The Russian beet salad was (tasty) than I had expected.

_____ **19.** The Italian gelato was the (incredible) ice cream I've ever tasted.

_____ **20.** I have never felt (full) in my entire life!

Notes for Home: Your child used comparative forms of adjectives to compare two things and superlative forms to compare three or more things. ***Home Activity:*** Look through pictures in magazines. Use comparative and superlative forms of adjectives to compare the pictures.

Adverbs

An **adverb** tells how, when, or where something happens. Most adverbs tell about verbs. An adverb can appear either before or after the verb. Many adverbs that tell how end in **-ly.**

How: The dancer performed <u>gracefully</u>.
(Other examples: <u>beautifully, slowly, carefully</u>)

Adverbs can also tell when or where an action happens.

When: Your new costume arrived <u>today</u>.
(Other examples: <u>always, first, last</u>)

Where: Don't leave it lying <u>around</u>.
(Other examples: <u>far, out, through</u>)

Directions: Underline the adverb or adverbs in each sentence.

1. Frank was doing poorly in school.

2. Then he suddenly improved.

3. In class, he always paid attention.

4. Frank waited hopefully for Awards Day.

5. He excitedly claimed his award as the Most Improved Student.

Directions: Write the adverb that tells more about each underlined verb.

_____ 6. That day, Frank quickly <u>ran</u> home.

_____ 7. He said he would never <u>forget</u> how much his parents had helped him.

_____ 8. Then he immediately <u>began</u> his homework.

_____ 9. Frank would <u>work</u> first.

_____ 10. He would have <u>fun</u> later.

Notes for Home: Your child identified adverbs—words that tell how, when, or where an action happens. *Home Activity:* Ask your child questions about the day's events. Invite your child to use adverbs in his or her answers.

Adverbs

Directions: Write whether each underlined adverb tells **when, where,** or **how.**

_____ 1. My brother and I <u>always</u> enjoyed old family stories.

_____ 2. We <u>eagerly</u> listened to tales about Korea.

_____ 3. My brother <u>sincerely</u> wanted to visit Korea.

_____ 4. Our parents said he could study <u>there</u>.

_____ 5. My brother <u>nervously</u> boarded the plane.

Directions: Write an adverb for each sentence that tells whatever is named in ( ). Write your adverb on the line to the left.

_____ 6. John's uncle _____ told him tales from Ireland. (when)

_____ 7. John liked _____ the stories about leprechauns. (how)

_____ 8. "If you leave milk for a leprechaun," one story said, "the grateful creature will _____ work for you." (how)

_____ 9. The Irish _____ call leprechauns "the little people." (when)

_____ 10. John thinks we could use some grateful leprechauns _____! (where)

Write a Letter

On a separate sheet of paper, write a letter telling about your family's culture to a pen pal. Describe an everyday event or a special holiday tradition. Use at least one adverb in each sentence.

Notes for Home: Your child identified adverbs telling how, when, or where something happened. *Home Activity:* Tell your child a story about something that happened in your family. Have your child identify each adverb and say which it tells: how, when, or where.

Adverbs

Circle the adverb that tells **how.**

1. My brother ate slowly.

Circle the adverb that tells **when.**

2. He finished dinner last.

Circle the adverb that tells **where.**

3. He left his dishes sitting out.

An **adverb** tells how, when, or where something happens. Most adverbs tell about verbs. An adverb can appear before or after the verb. Many adverbs that tell how end in **-ly.**

Directions: Underline the adverb in each sentence.

1. Today the bears explore their surroundings.

2. One cub runs outside.

3. The bear family plays happily.

4. They always leave their home.

5. They travel around.

6. The three cubs never leave their mother's side.

Directions: Write an adverb that tells more about each underlined verb.

_____ 7. The bears <u>hunt</u> for food.

_____ 8. Salmon <u>are swimming</u> toward their destination.

_____ 9. The mother <u>steps</u> into the stream.

Notes for Home: Your child identified and wrote adverbs in sentences. *Home Activity:* Talk with your child about what you did today. Have your child point out adverbs you use to describe how, when, or where.

Adverbs

Directions: Write whether each underlined adverb tells when, where, or how.

_____ **1.** Snakes don't come <u>here</u>.

_____ **2.** It is hard to <u>easily</u> find them in our town.

_____ **3.** You have to travel <u>far</u> if you want to see one.

_____ **4.** When you do spot one, you must walk <u>quietly</u>.

Directions: Write sentences, using a verb and an adverb from the box.

Verbs	Adverbs
move	quickly
run	slowly
talk	hard
eat	loudly
melt	last
try	silently

5. _____

6. _____

7. _____

8. _____

9. _____

10. _____

Notes for Home: Your child wrote adverbs in sentences. *Home Activity:* Have your student read a favorite story and look for adverbs. Then have him or her write new sentences with the adverbs from the story.

Adverbs

Directions: Identify the adverb or adverbs that tell about the underlined verb in each sentence. Write the adverb or adverbs on the line.

_____ 1. When I was little, my father often <u>told</u> me stories.

_____ 2. I got into bed and <u>waited</u> eagerly for my story.

_____ 3. My father sat on my bed and <u>spoke</u> softly.

_____ 4. Sometimes he <u>told</u> me made-up stories.

_____ 5. As I got older, though, he usually <u>told</u> real stories.

_____ 6. The stories I really <u>liked</u> were about my father as a boy.

_____ 7. As I <u>lay</u> there, I tried to picture him at that age.

_____ 8. Once, as a little boy, he <u>looked</u> outside and saw a red glow in the sky.

_____ 9. Thinking the world was on fire, he <u>ran</u> downstairs.

_____ 10. "You've seen your first sunset," his mother <u>said</u> to him gently.

Directions: Write the comparative or superlative form of the adverb in ( ) to complete each sentence.

_____ 11. "Please walk (fast)," said my brother.

_____ 12. We wanted to get to our grandparents' house (early) than our parents.

_____ 13. We arrived (soon) than anyone else, and we listened eagerly to my grandfather's wonderful stories.

_____ 14. I laughed (loudly) of all when he told us about our father's adventures as a boy.

_____ 15. When our parents arrived (late), we looked at my father and giggled.

Notes for Home: Your child identified adverbs—words that tell how, where, or when something happens—and wrote comparative and superlative adverbs. *Home Activity:* Talk with your child about a TV show. Ask questions using *how, when,* and *where.*

Using Adverbs to Improve Sentences

The sentence below does not paint a clear picture. It needs descriptive details.

The storyteller spoke.

One way to revise the sentence is by adding an adverb.

The storyteller spoke <u>quietly</u>. (tells how)
The storyteller spoke <u>later</u>. (tells when)
The storyteller spoke <u>outside</u>. (tells where)

Never use more adverbs than you need for expressing ideas clearly.

The storyteller spoke confidently, strongly, easily, and fast.

Directions: Add adverbs to make the sentences more interesting. For each sentence, supply the kind of adverb named in ( ). Write the adverb on the line to the left.

_____ 1. There is someone in our family who _____ likes telling family stories. (how)

_____ 2. Uncle Bruce will _____ tell a good story. (how)

_____ 3. I _____ like the stories about me as a baby. (when)

_____ 4. He _____ tells about our visit to the country. (when)

_____ 5. We rented a little house on a lake, and I learned to swim _____. (where)

_____ 6. My uncle used to hold me _____ in the water. (how)

_____ 7. One day he _____ let go of me in the water. (how)

_____ 8. _____ I was swimming! (when)

_____ 9. He enjoys seeing how _____ I swim now. (how)

_____ 10. _____ I will teach others how to swim. (when)

Notes for Home: Your child added adverbs to make sentences more interesting. ***Home Activity:*** Have your child tell you about his or her day. Ask questions your child can answer using adverbs.

Using Adverbs to Improve Sentences

Directions: Add an adverb to improve each sentence. Remember that an adverb can tell how, when, or where the action takes place. Write the new sentence with the adverb on the line.

1. Nellie's girlfriend wanted to go to a sleep over.

_____

_____

2. She explained, "My parents think I am too young."

_____

_____

3. Nellie told her parents she wanted to join her friends.

_____

_____

4. Nellie's mother answered her daughter.

_____

_____

5. She told Nellie, "Act grown-up, and we will allow you to go."

_____

_____

Write a Diary Entry

On a separate sheet of paper, write a diary entry. Tell about a time when you showed your family that you were grown-up enough to do something new. Use adverbs to tell how, when, or where things happened.

Notes for Home: Your child added adverbs to sentences. *Home Activity:* Play "Who Am I?" by taking turns describing familiar people, using adverbs to describe how they perform actions.

Using Adverbs to Improve Sentences

Choose a word from the box to finish each sentence.

now	outside	happily

Add an adverb that tells **how.**

1. The young cub played _____ .

Add an adverb that tells **when.**

2. He wanted to eat _____ .

Add an adverb that tells **where.**

3. Then he took a nap _____ .

One way to add descriptive detail to a sentence is by using an **adverb.** Adverbs can tell more about **how, when,** or **where** something happens. Do not use more adverbs than you need. Too many adverbs can make a sentence confusing.

Directions: Add descriptive detail to each sentence by choosing an adverb from the box. Write the adverb on the line.

later	quickly	gently	quietly	down

1. Water filled the cold pool _____ .

2. The bright sun melted the ice _____ .

3. Magda whispered _____ to her mother.

4. The trees bent _____ in the wind.

5. Our brown horse took us home _____ .

Notes for Home: Your child wrote adverbs in sentences. *Home Activity:* Write five verbs on cards. Have your child choose a card and write a sentence using that verb and any adverb that he or she would like to use.

© Scott Foresman 4

Using Adverbs to Improve Sentences

Directions: The verb is underlined in each sentence. Write the adverb that tells more about it.

1. The run <u>rises</u> first. _____

2. A bird <u>sings</u> clearly. _____

3. Next, the waves <u>break</u>. _____

4. The boat <u>sails</u> smoothly. _____

5. Sails <u>flap</u> slowly. _____

6. The wind <u>blows</u> there. _____

7. Sailors <u>work</u> carefully. _____

Directions: Find the adverb in each sentence. Then write it in the spaces next to the sentence.

8. The scientists work hard. ____ ____ □ ____

9. The boat moves fast. ____ □ ____ ____

10. The team works well. ____ ____ ____ □

11. The gulls dive quickly. ____ ____ ____ □ ____ ____ ____

12. The scientists watch quietly. ____ ____ ____ □ ____ ____ ____

Unscramble the letters in the squares and write the word that completes the sentence.

The captain speaks ____ ____ ____ ____ ____ l y .

Write a Deep-Sea Tale

On a separate sheet of paper, write about a sea creature. Use abverbs to give details about how the creature might move.

Notes for Home: Your child identified and wrote adverbs in sentences. *Home Activity:* Have your child explain to you the role of adverbs in sentences. (Adverbs tell more about the action named by the verb.)

© Scott Foresman 4

Name _____

Possessive Nouns and Pronouns

REVIEW

Directions: Make each underlined noun possessive. Write the possessive noun on the line.

1. that <u>car</u> color _____

2. the <u>people</u> choice _____

3. <u>Bess</u> bicycle _____

4. his <u>parents</u> automobile _____

5. the <u>child</u> tricycle _____

Directions: Underline each possessive pronoun. Write **S** above the pronoun if it is singular. Write **P** if it is plural.

6. Rosa, do you have your ticket to the car show?

7. My family drove there in our old jalopy.

8. Many people showed off their antique cars.

9. Tina found the car of her dreams.

10. Bryan, however, preferred his motorcycle.

Directions: Circle the correct word in ( ) to complete each sentence.

11. Does that red car belong to (you're/your) parents?

12. No, that is my cousin (Iris/Iris's) car.

13. She set up her (baby's/babies) car seat in the back.

14. The dog lies on (it's/its) pillow in the front.

15. Her passengers will have to look around for (they/their) own place to sit.

Notes for Home: Your child used possessive nouns and pronouns—nouns and pronouns that show ownership. *Home Activity:* Point to things around the house. Have your child use possessive nouns and pronouns to tell who owns each object.

Name _____

Pronouns

Pronouns are words that replace nouns or noun phrases. *I, you, he, she, it, me, him,* and *her* are singular pronouns. *We, you, they, us,* and *them* are plural pronouns. The singular pronoun *I* is always capitalized.

Scruffy likes to ride in the car.
<u>She</u> is the first to jump into <u>it</u> when <u>we</u> go for a drive.

Directions: Underline each singular pronoun once and each plural pronoun twice.

1. Jane said she wanted to bike all the way to Maine.

2. We told Jane the idea was foolish and dangerous.

3. Jane said it wasn't dangerous; five other high school students and two gym teachers would be in the group.

4. "Just call us if you find the trip too hard," Mom told Jane.

5. "Call me collect anytime," Dad added.

6. Jane just smiled. "I won't need to do it," she said.

7. "You say so *now*," Dad pointed out.

8. "I know you all mean well," Jane said.

9. "However, I am a big girl now, and we will be careful."

10. "Well, stay alert and be sure you call home every night," Mom directed.

Directions: Choose a pronoun in ( ) to replace each underlined noun or noun phrase. Write the pronoun on the line.

_____ 11. <u>Jane</u> did call us every night. (She/I)

_____ 12. She spoke to <u>Mom and Dad</u>. (us/them)

_____ 13. They gave <u>Jane</u> advice. (her/it)

_____ 14. Jane listened to <u>Mom</u>. (her/me)

_____ 15. Jane listened to <u>Dad</u> too. (them/him)

Notes for Home: Your child identified singular and plural pronouns and wrote pronouns. *Home Activity:* Name objects and people and have your child suggest pronouns for them.

© Scott Foresman 4

Pronouns

Directions: Choose a pronoun in ( ) to replace each underlined noun or noun phrase. Write the pronoun on the line.

_____ 1. I couldn't wait to go on vacation in <u>our new mobile home</u>. (it/them)

_____ 2. <u>Our next-door neighbors</u> had fun going on a trip last year. (We/They)

_____ 3. Somebody had given <u>our neighbors</u> many good suggestions. (us/them)

_____ 4. They passed the suggestions on to <u>my family and me</u>. (it/us)

_____ 5. <u>My family and I</u> made sure we didn't drive too far in a single day. (We/They)

_____ 6. <u>The trip</u> was very interesting. (I/It)

_____ 7. <u>Mom</u> found some shorter routes. (She/They)

_____ 8. <u>My brother</u> found campsites. (He/They)

_____ 9. <u>My sister</u> just had fun. (She/We)

_____ 10. <u>Mom and Dad</u> say that next year we'll feel like expert travelers. (We/They)

Write a Postcard

On a separate sheet of paper, write a postcard to a friend about a trip you have taken. The trip can be a real one or one you have imagined. Make sure you use some pronouns as well as nouns. Circle all the pronouns you use.

Notes for Home: Your child used pronouns to replace nouns. **Home Activity:** Think of one or more people or objects in the room. Give a pronoun, such as *they*, and play a questions game with your child to identify those people or objects.

Name _____

Amazing Alice!

Pronouns

RETEACHING

Read the sentences. Arrows connect each pronoun with a noun.

Eli plants <u>seeds</u>. <u>He</u> likes to plant <u>them</u>.

1. Write the pronoun that stands for the noun <u>Eli</u>. _____

2. Write the pronoun that stands for the noun <u>seeds</u>. _____

A **pronoun** takes the place of a noun or nouns. Singular pronouns are **I, you, she, he, it, me, her,** and **him.** Plural pronouns are **we, you, they, us,** and **them.**

Directions: Circle the pronoun in each sentence.

1. I carry some tools for Flo.

2. We ask the teacher for the small rake.

3. She does not have the rake.

4. Flo asks her for the vegetable seeds.

5. The teacher gives them to Flo.

Directions: Write the correct pronoun to stand for each underlined noun.

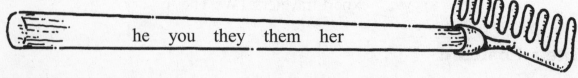

he   you   they   them   her

6. <u>Eli</u> planted seeds. _____ enjoyed the work.

7. <u>Janet</u> wanted to help. Eli gave _____ pepper seeds.

8. Janet took the <u>seeds</u>. She planted _____ in the ground.

9. <u>Bill and Tanya</u> watched. _____ held water buckets.

10. Eli said to <u>Tanya</u>, "Now _____ can water the plants."

Notes for Home: Your child identified and wrote pronouns in sentences. **Home Activity:** Read a news article with your child. Have him or her point out the pronouns and use three of them in new sentences.

© Scott Foresman 4

104 Pronouns

Pronouns

Directions: Circle six pronouns in the puzzle. Then write the pronouns in the sentences to replace the words in ( ).

h e r s s a
i s t h e y
m o h e i t

1. (Marla and Joe) live in the Painted Desert. _____

2. (The Painted Desert) is beautiful. _____

3. (Marla) likes the colors of the desert. _____

4. I bring (Marla) colored sand. _____

5. (Joe) likes the weather in the desert. _____

6. We ask (Joe) questions. _____

Directions: Write a pronoun to complete each sentence.

My family traveled to the Painted Desert. **7.** _____ marveled at the

animal life. Lizards and toads moved along the ground near **8.** _____ .

9. _____ are strange creatures. My father spotted some bats high

above **10.** _____ last night. **11.** _____ exclaimed,

12. "_____ watched **13.** _____ . **14.** _____ can fly

very fast!"

Write a Short Description

On a separate sheet of paper, write a short description of a place you have read about. Use pronouns in your sentences to avoid repeating nouns.

Notes for Home: Your child identified and wrote pronouns in sentences. *Home Activity:* Have your child write about a trip your family has taken. Challenge him or her to use pronouns to avoid repeating nouns.

Name _____

Pronouns

REVIEW

Directions: Underline each pronoun in the sentences below.

1. For years Ben and I hoped we could sail to America.

2. In 1919 the dream came true for us.

3. We grew up in a little Polish town, but now we were leaving it forever.

4. "I cannot say good-bye to you," sobbed Ben's mother.

5. Watching Ben leave for America was the hardest thing she had ever done.

Directions: Choose a pronoun in ( ) to replace the underlined noun or noun phrase in each sentence. Circle the pronoun you chose.

6. Ben and I were beginning a new life in New York City. (We/Us)

7. After our little Polish town, the city seemed so big. (they/it)

8. The size and the noise frightened Ben and me. (him/us)

9. Some people seemed nice, though, and we became friends with people. (you/them)

10. These people helped us find our way around. (They/It)

11. We did not know English, so we studied the language. (him/it)

12. Our friend Anna spoke English well, and Anna helped us study. (we/she)

13. Her husband was a tailor, and the husband found a job for Ben. (he/you)

14. We were so grateful to Anna and her husband. (them/us)

15. Life was still very hard, but life got better every day. (she/it)

© Scott Foresman 4

Notes for Home: Your child identified and used pronouns—words that take the place of nouns. *Home Activity:* Ask your child to tell you some jokes or funny stories. Help your child list the pronouns he or she uses.

Subject and Object Pronouns

Subject pronouns are pronouns that are used as the subjects of sentences.

Moesha and <u>I</u> like to travel.

Singular subject pronouns: I, you, he, she, it
Plural subject pronouns: we, you, they

Object pronouns follow action verbs.

Dan Nehmi's parents brought <u>him</u> to this country.

Singular object pronouns: me, you, him, her, it
Plural object pronouns: us, you, them

Directions: Circle the correct pronoun in ( ) to complete each sentence. Write **S** on the line if it is a subject pronoun. Write **O** if it is an object pronoun.

_____ **1.** My brother and (I/me) longed to go to America.

_____ **2.** (Us/We) heard people say newcomers quickly became rich.

_____ **3.** Our mother said not to believe (them/they).

_____ **4.** "But (us/you) must go and find out for yourselves."

_____ **5.** Our sister kissed both of (we/us).

_____ **6.** "Come with us," (I/me) said.

_____ **7.** "(I/You) want to stay here with our parents," my sister answered.

_____ **8.** Our father was sorry that we were leaving (him/he).

_____ **9.** "(Them/They) have a dream," our mother told him.

_____ **10.** "Someday you and (me/I) may live in America too."

Notes for Home: Your child chose subject and object pronouns to complete sentences. ***Home Activity:*** Say a sentence with nouns as subject and object: *Mrs. Nehmi told Dan about new customs.* Have your child replace the nouns with pronouns: *She told him about new customs.*

Subject and Object Pronouns

Directions: Choose the correct pronoun in ( ) to complete each sentence. Write the pronoun on the line.

_____ 1. Have (you/she) ever wondered what *success* really means?

_____ 2. The best way to define (it/her) is by giving examples.

_____ 3. At first, Amy was afraid of the water, but then (her/she) learned how to swim.

_____ 4. Luis decided to get 100% on his test, and (he/they) did.

_____ 5. The twins earned enough money, so their parents let (them/they) go to summer camp.

_____ 6. Ms. Chang convinced her boss to give (she/her) a better job.

_____ 7. Aaron's little brother couldn't catch a ball, so Aaron showed (he/him) how.

_____ 8. Laura and Sandy were confused about math, so they asked Mr. Franklin to help (him/them).

_____ 9. Some people think success means being rich and famous, but (they/it) may be wrong.

_____ 10. Now that you've read these examples, what do (they/you) think?

Write an Ad

On a separate sheet of paper, write a Back-to-School ad listing the "Top 5" ways to have success in school. Use both subject pronouns and object pronouns. Underline the pronouns in your ad.

Notes for Home: Your child replaced nouns with subject pronouns such as: *I, we, you, he, she, it,* and *they* or object pronouns such as: *me, us, you, him, her, it,* and *them.* **Home Activity:** Together, read about a famous person. Ask your child to identify the subject and object pronouns.

© Scott Foresman 4

Subject and Object Pronouns

Read each pair of sentences. Write a pronoun on each line.

1. A clown and a dog came to school. _____ performed tricks.

2. The dog was good at jumping. The class liked watching _____ .

A **subject pronoun** is used in the subject of a sentence. Subject pronouns are **I, you, she, he, it, we,** and **they.** An object pronoun is used in the predicate of a sentence or in a prepositional phrase. Object pronouns are **me, you, him, her, it, us,** and **them.**

Directions: Circle the subject pronoun in each sentence. Then write it on the line.

1. I have learned many facts about space from Mr. Turner. _____

2. He taught the class how to spot a shooting star. _____

3. It is difficult for my sister to do. _____

4. She will be in Mr. Turner's class in three years. _____

5. One day we will watch shooting stars together. _____

6. They are beautiful to see! _____

Directions: Circle the object pronoun in each sentence. Then write it on the line.

7. Mark gave her a drawing of the Big Dipper. _____

8. Did Mark give you a picture too? _____

9. Mr. Gomez gave us star maps. _____

10. Mr. Gomez keeps them in the classroom. _____

11. The star map fascinates me. _____

12. Nina and Leon looked at it carefully. _____

Notes for Home: Your child identified subject and object pronouns in sentences. *Home Activity:* Together, read an article in a newspaper. Have your child circle three subject or object pronouns. Then have him or her write new sentences, using pronouns from the article.

© Scott Foresman 4

Subject and Object Pronouns

Directions: Read the paragraph. Then circle the correct pronoun in ( ) that completes each sentence. Remember:

- **Subject pronouns** are used as subjects in a sentence:
    I, you, he, she, it, we, and **they.**
- **Object pronouns** are used after action verbs:
    me, you, him, her, it, us, and **them.**

1.–8.

Grandma invited Tim and (I, me) to spend the holidays with her. Mom and Dad drove (we, us) to the airport. (They, Them) waved as the plane took off into the sky. (We, Us) slept on the plane. A flight attendant had to wake (I, me) up when we landed. (He, Him) carried our bags off the plane. Grandma seemed really excited to see (we, us). (She, Her) had balloons for each of us!

Write a Travel Journal

Write about a trip you would like to take with a friend or a book character. It might be a trip to a place in your town or a trip to a faraway place. Check to make sure you used subject and object pronouns correctly in your description.

Notes for Home: Your child identified subject and object pronouns in a paragraph. *Home Activity:* Have your child reread his or her travel journal. Then ask your child to circle the subject pronouns and underline the object pronouns that he or she wrote.

Subject and Object Pronouns

Directions: Underline the pronoun in each sentence. Write **S** above the pronoun if it is a subject pronoun. Write **O** if it is an object pronoun.

1. Dolores told me about the thirteenth-century explorer Marco Polo.

2. She had just read a book about this young traveler.

3. At the age of seventeen, he and two family members set out on a long journey.

4. The trip took them from Italy to China, through deserts, mountains, and wondrous cities.

5. It was a difficult journey in 1271, lasting four years.

Directions: Choose the pronoun in ( ) that completes each sentence. Circle the pronoun you chose.

6. Julia and (I/me) are writing a report about the Vikings.

7. (They/Them) were also known as Norsemen.

8. Their swift ships carried (they/them) far from their homes in Norway, Sweden, and Denmark.

9. (They/Them) sailed to North America more than a thousand years ago.

10. (We/Us) read about Leif Ericson, one of their leaders.

11. (He/Him) may have been the first European to reach North America.

12. The land pleased (he/him), and he named it Vinland.

13. The Vikings really interested Julia and (I/me).

14. One thing puzzled (she/her), though.

15. (Her/She) wondered why Christopher Columbus was so much more famous than Leif Ericson.

© Scott Foresman 4

Notes for Home: Your child used the pronouns *I, we, you, he, she, it,* and *they* as subjects and *me, us, you, him, her,* and *them* as objects of verbs. **Home Activity:** Together, look for pronouns in a magazine. Decide whether each is a subject or an object pronoun.

Name_____

Pronouns and Referents

Pronouns get most of their meaning from the nouns or noun phrases they replace. The noun that a pronoun replaces is its **referent.** It names the person, place, or thing to which the pronoun refers. In the following sentences, the referents are underlined once, and the pronouns are underlined twice.

<u>Jo</u> wants to be an explorer when <u>she</u> grows up.

Soon, <u>Jo and Pavel</u> will visit the Gobi Desert. <u>They</u> can hardly wait!

A pronoun and its referent must agree. In the first example sentence above, the singular subject pronoun *she* agrees with its referent, the singular subject *Jo.* In the next example sentences, the plural subject pronoun *They* agrees with its referent, the compound subject *Jo and Pavel.*

Directions: Match the pronoun with the noun phrase that could be its referent. Write the letter of the referent on the line.

_____ **1.** we   **a.** Mr. Chin

_____ **2.** they   **b.** airplane

_____ **3.** she   **c.** Maggie

_____ **4.** it   **d.** Tony and Sari

_____ **5.** he   **e.** Dad and I

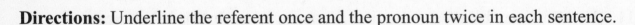

Directions: Underline the referent once and the pronoun twice in each sentence.

6. Pavel and Jo can't wait until they go to Nepal.

7. The journey will be long, but it will be fun.

8. Pavel has a new guidebook that will help him.

9. The tickets are expensive, but they are worth the price!

10. Pavel went to Nepal last year. It was beautiful.

Notes for Home: Your child connected pronouns to the words to which they refer. *Home Activity:* Read a story together and look for nouns and pronouns. For each pronoun, name the noun it replaces.

Pronouns and Referents

Directions: Circle the correct pronoun in ( ) to complete each sentence. The referents for the pronouns are underlined to help you.

1. Long ago, <u>navigators</u> steering ships had only the stars to guide (he/them).

2. The <u>stars</u> look different when you view (it/them) from different parts of the world.

3. <u>Navigation</u> takes a long time to learn, but you may find (it/you) worthwhile.

4. <u>Sailors</u> who want to be coastal pilots know (it/they) must learn navigation.

5. <u>Luisa and I</u> have decided that (she/we) will sail around the world someday.

Directions: Revise each sentence. Use pronouns to avoid repeating a noun. Cross out nouns and write new pronouns above the nouns. Circle the referent for each pronoun you used.

6. Explorers have interesting lives because explorers often visit new places.

7. Ferdinand Magellan became famous when Ferdinand Magellan sailed around the globe.

8. Luisa plans to sail around the world when Luisa grows up.

9. Luisa will be our navigator because Luisa has been studying navigation.

10. Sacajawea was the guide for Lewis and Clark. Without Sacajawea, Lewis and Clark would have been lost.

Write an Adventure Story

On a separate sheet of paper, write the story of an explorer. The explorer may be a real person that you know about or an imaginary one. Use at least five pronouns that have referents. When you are finished, identify the referent for each pronoun.

Notes for Home: Your child used pronouns to improve sentences and identified the nouns that the pronouns replaced. *Home Activity:* Write a few sentences that include pronouns. Ask your child to identify the noun each pronoun replaces.

Pronouns and Referents

A referent is a noun or noun phrase that gets replaced by a pronoun.

The referent is underlined. Circle the pronoun that replaces the referent.

<u>Linnea and Jack</u> are hungry before they eat dinner.

A **pronoun** gets most of its meaning from the noun or noun phrase it replaces. Its **referent** names the person, place, or thing to which the pronoun refers.

Directions: Circle the pronoun in each sentence. Write each referent on the line.

_____ **1.** Walter told Mrs. Chan he would water the plants.

_____ **2.** Mrs. Chan explained how she would like the plants to be watered.

_____ **3.** Many plants from stores come with information about what they need to survive.

_____ **4.** A friend sent a picture he had taken of redwood trees.

_____ **5.** The picture was beautiful, and it showed how large the trees were.

Directions: Match the pronoun with the noun or noun phrase that could be its referent. Write the letter of the referent on the line.

_____ **6.** he   **a.** Linda

_____ **7.** we   **b.** Jonathan and Chris

_____ **8.** they   **c.** the truck

_____ **9.** it   **d.** Pierre

_____ **10.** she   **e.** Flora and I

Notes for Home: Your child identified pronouns and their referents—the nouns or noun phrases to which pronouns refer. *Home Activity:* Together, write a poem about your family. Use at least three pronouns and their referents.

Pronouns and Referents

Directions: Underline the four pronouns in the paragraph. Then list the referents on the lines below.

Carlos studied the five senses with Mrs. Katz. She knows many things about the sense organs. They are the ears, nose, eyes, tongue, and skin. Carlos added a fact about the brain. It works with the eyes. Together they help people to see.

1. _____ 2. _____ 3. _____ 4. _____

Directions: Rewrite each sentence. Use a pronoun to replace the underlined referent.

5. Ned and Liz needed a volunteer for an experiment.

   _____

6. Liz used a handkerchief for a blindfold.

   _____

7. Ned moved an alarm clock around the room.

   _____

8. The clock ticked softly at a distance.

   _____

9. Now and then Liz asked about the clock.

   _____

10. Volunteers pointed to the sound.

    _____

Write Sentences About Senses

Close your eyes and listen to the sounds around you. Then, on a separate sheet of paper, write sentences about what you heard. Use pronouns and referents in some of your sentences.

Notes for Home: Your child identified pronouns and referents in sentences. *Home Activity:* Have your child write sentences about his or her friends. Challenge your child to use at least three pronouns and their referents.

© Scott Foresman 4

Pronouns and Referents

Directions: Underline the pronoun in each sentence. Then draw a circle around its referent. Hint: One pronoun is a possessive pronoun.

1. Turtles may seem slow and dull, but they are really interesting creatures.

2. Jeff and Josh like turtles so much that they have a pet turtle.

3. Jeff claims that he has trained the turtle to do tricks.

4. The turtle's only "trick," though, is to pull its head inside the shell.

5. Jeff says that seems like an amazing trick to him!

Directions: Write a sentence or a pair of sentences using the nouns and pronouns given. Use each noun as the referent of each pronoun.

6. turtle, it

_____

7. students, they

_____

_____

8. teacher, him

_____

_____

9. scientist, she

_____

10. turtles, them

_____

Notes for Home: Your child matched pronouns with their referents—the nouns or noun phrases they replace in sentences. ***Home Activity:*** With your child, write a story about an animal. Then ask your child to identify the referent of each pronoun in the story.

Prepositions and Prepositional Phrases

A **preposition** is a word that shows how a word is related to other words in the sentence. A preposition begins a group of words called a **prepositional phrase.** The phrase ends with a noun or pronoun called the **object of the preposition.**

The turtle walked <u>into the (sea.)</u> The plane flew <u>above the (sea.)</u>

A prepositional phrase can be used to tell where, when, how, or which one.

Where did the turtle go? It went <u>into the sea</u>.

When did it go? It moved <u>after sunset</u>.

How did it walk? It walked <u>with slow steps</u>.

Which turtle was it? It was the one <u>with a spotted shell</u>.

Common Prepositions				
about	around	between	into	to
above	at	by	of	under
across	behind	for	on	upon
after	below	from	over	with
against	beneath	in	through	without

Directions: Underline the prepositional phrase in each sentence once. Draw a second line under the preposition.

1. The dolphins leaped over the waves.

2. They liked playing in the water.

3. At certain times, they joined the tuna.

4. Many tiny fish swam into view.

5. A baby dolphin swam after them.

6. The crabs walked on the shore.

7. Some hid under the mud.

8. Some dug in the sand.

9. One crab with a heavy shell moved slowly.

10. Another climbed over the log.

Notes for Home: Your child used prepositions, such as *in, on,* and *with,* and prepositional phrases, such as *in the sea.* **Home Activity:** Ask your child to tell you the exact location of an object that you name. Then ask the child to identify the prepositions he or she used.

© Scott Foresman 4

Prepositions and Prepositional Phrases

Directions: Circle the prepositional phrase that best answers the question in ( ) to complete each sentence.

1. Huge mammals called whales live _____. *(Where?)*
   (in the ocean/on land and sea)

2. This has been their home _____. *(When?)*
   (for the future/for a long time)

3. Blue whales, killer whales, and others exist _____. *(Where?)*
   (on our planet/on small ponds)

4. Some countries protect whales _____. *(How?)*
   (through laws/from wild animals)

5. Whales _____ perform well in water shows. *(Which?)*
   (with kind trainers/without experience)

Directions: Add a prepositional phrase to each sentence. Begin the phrase with a preposition from the box.

for	to	at	into	toward

6. Rosa dived happily _____.

7. She swam until her dad waved _____.

8. Her dad was pointing _____.

9. Rosa suddenly felt hungry _____.

10. She waved back and swam _____.

Write Directions

On a separate sheet of paper, write directions telling how to get to a place that you like to visit. Use at least five prepositions, and underline each one.

Notes for Home: Your child wrote prepositions, such as *in, for,* and *through,* and prepositional phrases, such as *in the ocean.* **Home Activity:** Describe an object's location, using prepositions. Have your child guess the object and identify the prepositions you used.

© Scott Foresman 4

Prepositions and Prepositional Phrases

Choose the preposition in ( ) that makes the most sense in each sentence.

1. We ran (under/down) the path.

2. T.J. called (after/against) you left.

A **preposition** shows how a word is related to one or more other words in the sentence. A preposition is the first word in a **prepositional phrase.** Prepositional phrases can answer the questions **Where? When? How?** and **Which one?** What questions do the two sentences above answer?

Directions: Draw a line from the phrase on the left to the prepositional phrase on the right that best matches it.

1. Luz told Julie to go   from the basement

2. Their mother called   in the jar."

3. "There is money   after this show."

4. "I will go   by four o'clock!"

5. "Be back   to the store.

Directions: Underline the prepositional phrase or phrases in each sentence.

6. My dog is the best dog in the world.

7. He comes when I call, and he walks behind me.

8. If I go to the park, he comes with me.

9. One time I couldn't find him anywhere around the house.

10. I looked under the stairs.

11. I also searched through my bedroom.

Notes for Home: Your child identified prepositions and prepositional phrases in sentences. *Home Activity:* Look for prepositional phrases in books or magazines. Have your child identify which questions—*How? When? Where? Which one?*—they answer.

Prepositions and Prepositional Phrases

about	above	across	against	behind	by	in	through	to	under	with

Directions: Choose a preposition from the box to complete each sentence. Write it on the line to the left.

_____ 1. Last weekend my family went _____ a movie.

_____ 2. The movie was _____ a lot of animals.

_____ 3. The animals lived _____ a forest.

_____ 4. Some of them liked to hide _____ the dirt.

_____ 5. Others swung in trees _____ the ground.

_____ 6. My favorites were squirrels that ran _____ tree branches.

_____ 7. Sometimes they flew right _____ the leaves!

_____ 8. They never crashed _____ anything!

_____ 9. My younger stepsister hid _____ her mom.

_____ 10. She was afraid of the fox _____ sharp teeth.

Directions: Add a prepositional phrase to each sentence. Use a preposition from the box above to begin each prepositional phrase.

11. Kenji hid _____

12. He didn't want to be seen _____

13. His friends looked _____

14. One of them saw movement _____

15. Kenji was hiding _____

Notes for Home: Your child wrote prepositions and prepositional phrases. *Home Activity:* Have your child hide four objects in a room. Then have him or her write prepositional phrases as clues for you to find the objects.

© Scott Foresman 4

Compound and Complex Sentences

Directions: Write **compound** or **complex** to identify each kind of sentence.

_____ **1.** Our solar system has nine planets, but it has other parts as well.

_____ **2.** Asteroids are numerous, and some come near Earth.

_____ **3.** When an asteroid enters Earth's atmosphere, it is called a *meteor.*

_____ **4.** If it reaches Earth's surface, it is called a *meteorite.*

_____ **5.** Comets seem to have tails, but these are just trails of gas and dust.

_____ **6.** Because the Sun produces both heat and light, it is called a star.

_____ **7.** Mercury is the closest planet to the Sun, and Venus is the second closest planet.

_____ **8.** Pluto is thought to be the farthest planet, but there may be more planets beyond it.

Directions: Combine each pair of sentences. Add a connecting word, such as *and, but, or, because, if,* or *when,* to make the kind of sentence shown in ( ). Write your new sentence on the line.

9. Jupiter is the largest planet. It rotates very fast for its size. (compound)

_____

_____

10. Mercury is close to the Sun. It moves around the Sun in only 88 days. (complex)

_____

_____

 Notes for Home: Your child wrote compound and complex sentences. *Home Activity:* With your child, write simple sentences about space travel. Work together to try to combine them into compound or complex sentences.

Conjunctions

Connecting words like *and, but,* or *or* are called **conjunctions.** Conjunctions can be used to join words, phrases, or entire sentences. They are used to make compound subjects, predicates, and sentences.

Compound subject: Mercury <u>and</u> Venus are closest to the Sun.
Compound predicate: The probe circled the planet <u>and</u> sent signals.
Compound sentence: We can explore Venus, <u>or</u> we can explore Mars.

- Use *and* to join related ideas: Saturn <u>and</u> Uranus have rings.
- Use *but* to join contrasting ideas: Saturn's rings go around the planet, <u>but</u> Uranus's rings go over it.
- Use *or* to suggest a choice: Would you rather study Saturn <u>or</u> Uranus?

Directions: Underline the conjunction in each sentence.

1. Telescopes and microscopes provide useful information.

2. They have been used to study large and small objects.

3. Would you rather use a telescope or a microscope to look at the moon?

4. A telescope is good for looking at planets, but a microscope is better for looking at germs!

5. An astronomer uses a telescope, but a doctor uses a microscope.

Directions: Choose the conjunction in ( ) to complete each sentence. Write the conjunction on the line.

_____ 6. The probe sent back pictures (but/and) information.

_____ 7. Was the information new (or/but) old?

_____ 8. Some of the information was old, (but/or) most of it was new.

_____ 9. Both Mercury (and/but) the moon have craters.

_____ 10. We knew about the moon's craters, (but/or) we did not know about the craters on Mercury.

Notes for Home: Your child used the conjunctions *and, or,* and *but.* **Home Activity:** Say some sentences that include *and, or,* or *but.* Ask your child to identify the conjunctions and to describe the words, phrases, or sentences that each conjunction joins.

Conjunctions

Directions: Circle the correct conjunction in ( ) to complete each sentence.

1. The scientist looked through the telescope, (and/or) then she scratched her head.

2. Was something wrong with her telescope, (but/or) had she made a great discovery?

3. She blinked (and/or) then peered again at an object on the side of the planet.

4. It did not exactly twinkle, (or/but) it did look like a star!

5. The scientist was excited, (but/or) she decided to stay calm.

6. She called in a friend, (and/or) he thought he saw the same thing.

7. Was it a new star, (and/or) was it just something unimportant?

8. Would they become famous, (and/but) would other scientists respect them?

9. Together, she (and/or) he made an embarrassing but important discovery.

10. A space probe, on its way to explore the riverbeds (but/and) rocks of Mars, was what they had seen.

Write a Note

Imagine planning a long journey to explore a vast place, such as the ocean floor. On a separate sheet of paper, list the things that you would bring on your journey. Then write a note to yourself so you will remember to take those items. Use conjunctions to join words, phrases, and sentences.

© Scott Foresman 4

Notes for Home: Your child used *and, or,* and *but* to join words, phrases, and sentences. *Home Activity:* Say each conjunction and ask your child to say a sentence that includes it. Then invite the child to name a conjunction, and you offer a sentence that includes it.

Name _____

Conjunctions

Conjunctions can be used to join words, phrases, or sentences. Choose the conjunction **and, but,** or **or** to complete each sentence.

Example A: Marta _____ Sean enjoy soccer.

Example B: Sean likes to be the goalie, _____ Marta likes to play offense.

Example C: After a game, both friends drink a glass of lemonade _____ orange juice.

Conjunctions can be used to form compound subjects (Example A), compound predicates (Example C), and compound sentences (Example B).

Use **and** to join related ideas. Use **but** to join contrasting ideas. Use **or** to suggest a choice.

Directions: Choose the conjunction in ( ) that best completes each sentence. Write the conjunction on the line.

_____ **1.** Tara (and/but) Jack raked the garden.

_____ **2.** They were going to plant seeds (but/and) weed the garden.

_____ **3.** Jack wanted to plant vegetables, (but/or) Tara wanted to plant flowers.

_____ **4.** They realized that they didn't have to choose one (and/or) the other.

_____ **5.** Both friends made space in the garden for flowers (and/but) vegetables.

_____ **6.** The garden would be small, (or/but) it didn't matter.

Notes for Home: Your child identified and wrote the conjunctions *and, but,* and *or* in sentences. *Home Activity:* Write the words *and, but,* and *or* on cards. Have your child pick a card and make up a sentence with that conjunction.

© Scott Foresman 4

Conjunctions

Directions: Underline the conjunction in each sentence.

1. Oceans and lakes have many things in common.

2. They are bodies of water, and they contain fish.

3. You can swim in an ocean or in a lake.

4. You can also go fishing in oceans and lakes.

5. The biggest difference is that lakes have fresh water, but oceans have salt water.

Directions: Finish each sentence by adding the conjunction **and, but,** or **or,** and more information. Write the conjunction on the line.

6. Last week my friends _____

7. They were very excited _____

8. My father said I could either _____

9. I wanted to do both _____

10. Today I am going to the park _____

Write a Journal Entry

On a separate sheet of paper, write about a time you had to choose between doing two different things. Use at least three conjunctions.

© Scott Foresman 4

Notes for Home: Your child identified conjunctions and wrote them in sentences. *Home Activity:* Have your child explain to you the job of each conjunction in a sentence (*and*—joins related ideas; *but*—joins contrasting ideas; *or*—shows a choice).

Conjunctions

REVIEW

Directions: Choose the correct conjunction in ( ) to complete each sentence. Write the conjunction on the line.

_____ **1.** It is getting late, (but/or) I want to hear the next band.

_____ **2.** The guitar player (and/but) the keyboard player walked onto the stage together.

_____ **3.** Would the singer (and/or) the drummer be the next one onstage?

_____ **4.** The group played two old hits (and/but) two brand-new songs.

_____ **5.** Should we leave now (but/or) listen to another band?

Directions: Use the conjunction *and, but,* or *or* to combine each pair of sentences. Write your new sentence on the line.

6. The concert was almost sold out. We did get two tickets.

_____

_____

7. Can your brother drive us? Should we take the bus?

_____

8. The opening band was terrible. We know the second band will be great.

_____

_____

9. The band ran onstage. The crowd went wild.

_____

10. They opened with their biggest hit. The audience sang along.

_____

Notes for Home: Your child used the conjunctions *and, but,* and *or* to complete or combine sentences. *Home Activity:* Give your child two words and a conjunction. Challenge your child to form a sentence. Repeat as many times as you like.

© Scott Foresman 4

Sentences and Punctuation

A **sentence** is a group of words that makes a statement, a question, a command, a request, or an exclamation. It begins with a capital letter and ends with a punctuation mark. One way to tell whether a group of words is a complete sentence is to check whether it expresses a complete thought.

A **declarative sentence** is a sentence that makes a statement. It ends with a period.

I love music.

An **interrogative sentence** asks a question. It ends with a question mark.

Do you love music too?

An **imperative sentence** gives a command or a request. It ends with a period. The first word is usually a verb, or *please* followed by a verb. The subject *(you)* is not shown, but it is understood.

Listen to me play the guitar.

An **exclamatory sentence** shows strong feeling. It ends with an exclamation point.

That was so wonderful!

Directions: Match each group of words on the left with a group of words on the right to form complete sentences. Write the letter on the line.

_____ **1.** Did you go   **a.** study for a long time.

_____ **2.** At the concert,   **b.** was so talented!

_____ **3.** The lead guitarist   **c.** to the concert last week?

_____ **4.** I'm going   **d.** to start taking lessons next week.

_____ **5.** Good musicians must   **e.** the singer sang a solo.

Directions: Write the correct end punctuation on the line after each sentence.

6. Martin was practicing piano all afternoon _____

7. Did you know he is playing in the concert _____

8. Wow, he is a great musician _____

9. Why didn't he send me an invitation _____

10. I hope I can go to the concert _____

Notes for Home: Your child reviewed sentences and their end punctuation. *Home Activity:* Say a sentence and have your child punctuate it with a gesture: pointing a finger for a period, shaking his or her head for a question mark, and clapping hands for an exclamation mark.

Sentences and Punctuation

Directions: Write **S** on the line if each group of words is a sentence. Write **NS** if the group of words is not a sentence.

_____ **1.** I have been studying music since I was seven years old.

_____ **2.** For three years!

_____ **3.** The very first instrument I ever studied was.

_____ **4.** Then I decided to learn piano, so that I could play by myself.

_____ **5.** The reason I like to play solos?

Directions: Rewrite each sentence with correct capitalization and end punctuation.

6. do you think that it's better to play music by yourself

_____

7. if you could play any instrument in the world, what would it be

_____

8. my piano teacher wants me to study harder

_____

9. come to my concert and watch me play

_____

10. wow, I really love music

_____

Write a Description of Music

On a separate sheet of paper, write a description of some music that you like.
Explain why you like it and tell how the music makes you feel.

Notes for Home: Your child reviewed sentences and their end punctuation. **Home Activity:**
Have your child read aloud from a favorite story. Encourage your child to use his or her voice
to express statements, commands, questions, and exclamations.

Sentences and Punctuation   RETEACHING

A **sentence** is a group of words that makes a statement, a question, a command, a request, or an exclamation. It begins with a capital letter and ends with a punctuation mark.

Read each sentence. Write a punctuation mark that best completes each sentence.

1. Please bring me the book _____

2. I've never seen anything so amazing _____

3. Do you know what time it is _____

4. I am writing a report _____

An **imperative sentence** gives a command or makes a request and ends with a period. An **exclamatory sentence** shows strong feeling and ends with an exclamation point. An **interrogative sentence** asks a question and ends with a question mark. A **declarative sentence** makes a statement and ends with a period.

Directions: Read each sentence and identify which type it is. Write **declarative**, **exclamatory**, **imperative**, or **interrogative** on the line.

_____   1. What an exciting movie that was!

_____   2. Do you know the names of the actors?

_____   3. Yes, I do.

_____   4. Please tell me what they are.

_____   5. Can you wait until we get home?

_____   6. Tell me now.

_____   7. You are the most curious person I've ever met!

Notes for Home: Your child correctly punctuated four types of sentences. *Home Activity:* Write some sentences without end punctuation. Discuss with your child which punctuation mark (. or ! or ?) best ends each sentence.

Sentences and Punctuation

Directions: Write the correct end punctuation on the line after each sentence.

1. Everyone loved the play _____

2. Did Sabrina remember all her lines _____

3. Did you help clean up after the show _____

4. What a mess it was _____

5. Hang your costume in the closet _____

6. Phil fixed a light _____

7. Wow, what bright lights they are _____

8. Please fold all those chairs _____

9. Did you check down that row _____

10. Brenda swept the stage _____

11. Does Mr. Carter think we did well _____

12. He took everyone out for a snack _____

Directions: Rewrite each sentence with correct capitalization and end punctuation.

13. did you get tickets to the baseball game

_____

14. please get one for me too

_____

15. it will be a fun game

_____

16. what a great time we're going to have

_____

Notes for Home: Your child correctly punctuated four types of sentences. **Home Activity:** Listen to a favorite song. Have your child write some of the words to the song and decide which type of punctuation mark (. or ! or ?) to use.

© Scott Foresman 4

Proper Nouns and Adjectives

Directions: Rewrite each sentence correctly. Capitalize the proper nouns and adjectives.

1. ms. sams talked about the art of native peoples of north america.

_____

2. Groups in the great plains, such as the sioux, decorated with beads.

_____

3. In the united states, ancient stone dwellings are found in the southwest.

_____

4. Hundreds of families lived in these dwellings in arizona and new mexico.

_____

5. The american museum of natural history has a fine collection of native art.

_____

6. Have you seen any mexican art?

_____

7. Mexican art is another kind of american art.

_____

8. Many items show a spanish influence.

_____

9. Art is important to canadian groups too.

_____

10. For example, inuit sculptures are world famous.

_____

Notes for Home: Your child capitalized proper nouns and proper adjectives. *Home Activity:* Ask your child to write a paragraph about a place he or she would like to visit. Encourage your child to use proper nouns and adjectives in the paragraph.

Capitalization

Use these rules for **capitalization:**

- Capitalize the first word of a sentence.

<u>M</u>y friend is an artist.

- Capitalize the first word and every important word of a proper noun. Remember, proper nouns name particular persons, places, or things.

His name is <u>J</u>oseph <u>S</u>tephens.   He wrote a book called <u>*How to Paint*</u>.

- Capitalize the first letter of an abbreviation. An abbreviation is a shortened form of a word. It usually ends with a period. State name abbreviations use two capital letters and no periods.

He lives in <u>F</u>lagstaff, <u>AZ</u>.   His address is 182 <u>C</u>ottonwood <u>St</u>.

- Capitalize titles before people's names.

<u>C</u>apt. Alice Stephens is his wife.

Directions: Rewrite each sentence, using correct capitalization.

1. mrs. johnson is a very good artist.

_____

2. she lives in phoenix, az, in a big house.

_____

3. her address is 17 bluebird road.

_____

4. she teaches a class called "drawing can be fun!"

_____

5. she has visited all 50 states, including alaska and hawaii.

_____

Notes for Home: Your child practiced capitalizing proper nouns, abbreviations, and titles. *Home Activity:* Write down the names and addresses of some of your child's friends and relatives, without capitalizing them. Help him or her to capitalize each word correctly.

Capitalization

Directions: Write **C** on the line for each group of words that is correctly capitalized. If a group of words is not correctly capitalized, rewrite it on the line, using correct capitalization.

_____ 1. she created a new painting.

_____ 2. Capt. Martin Anderson

_____ 3. yuma, az

_____ 4. *The Life of the buffalo*

_____ 5. mr. peter alvarez

_____ 6. 1313 Blue View Terrace

_____ 7. los angeles, ca

Directions: Rewrite each sentence on the line, using proper capitalization.

8. frank has been an artist all his life.

_____

9. his best friend is dr. russell mears.

_____

10. together they wrote a book, called *we are native americans.*

_____

Write a Review

On a separate sheet of paper, write a review of a movie, book, or video you liked. Compare it to at least two other works. Remember to capitalize each proper noun you use in your review.

Notes for Home: Your child practiced capitalizing proper nouns, abbreviations, and titles. *Home Activity:* Write down some silly titles for books, movies, or videos without capitalizing them. Have your child correct the capitalizations.

Capitalization

Underline the sentence that is capitalized correctly.

1. I live at 2121 Dobson Ave.

2. my favorite book is called *cats and dogs*.

Use a **capital letter** to begin a **sentence.** Capitalize the first word and every important word of a **proper noun.** Proper nouns can be persons, places, or things. Capitalize the first letter of an **abbreviation.** Also capitalize **titles** before people's names.

Directions: Capitalize each sentence correctly and write it on the line.

1. i live at 1501 kenmore st.

_____

2. my sister turned six years old on may 6, 2000.

_____

3. dr. peter montgomery is my dentist.

_____

Directions: Write **correct** on the line next to each group of words that is capitalized correctly. Rewrite the others on the line, using correct capitalization.

_____ **4.** mrs. joanna thornton

_____ **5.** December 31, 1902

_____ **6.** the book *How I learned italian*

_____ **7.** Boston, Massachusetts

_____ **8.** he likes to write songs.

Notes for Home: Your child practiced capitalizing proper nouns, abbreviations, and titles. *Home Activity:* Have your child explain rules for using capital letters when writing.

Capitalization

Directions: Look at each underlined word or group of words. Some of them have mistakes. Find twelve capitalization mistakes in the paragraph. Rewrite the incorrect words, using capital letters correctly.

<u>my</u> friend <u>mr. Applebee</u> has lived on <u>town square st.</u> for a long time. He has been teaching me how to play the piano since last <u>march</u>. He teaches kids from other families in <u>harpersville</u> too. On <u>september 12</u>, we will have a <u>recital</u>. Everyone in the town will be there, including <u>capt. Maria Lopez</u> from the police department. I am a little nervous, but <u>mrs. applebee</u> told me not to be scared. <u>she</u> gave me a book called <u>*Your first recital*</u> by <u>r. j. Martin</u>. <u>now</u> I'm ready!

1. _____   7. _____

2. _____   8. _____

3. _____   9. _____

4. _____   10. _____

5. _____   11. _____

6. _____   12. _____

Directions: Rewrite each sentence, using correct capitalization.

13. rita and tony are going to visit their aunt and uncle.

_____

14. aunt gina and uncle andrew live in atlanta, georgia.

_____

15. they are planning to visit the fernbank museum of natural history.

_____

16. they haven't seen their aunt and uncle since january two years ago!

_____

Notes for Home: Your child corrected mistakes in capitalization. *Home Activity:* Write (without capital letters) a list of titles and authors of books your child has read. Have him or her capitalize the titles and authors correctly.

Compound Subjects and Objects

Directions: Combine each set of sentences by using a compound subject. Write your new sentence on the lines. (Remember, verbs must agree with the subject.)

1. Harlem is located in New York City. Greenwich Village is located in New York City also.

_____

_____

2. Many workers settled in Harlem in the 1920s. Many artists settled there too.

_____

_____

3. Writers made Harlem the center of African American culture. Musicians and artists did too.

_____

_____

Directions: Combine each set of sentences by using a compound object. Write your new sentence on the lines.

4. Musicians from the South brought jazz to Harlem. They brought other exciting music as well.

_____

_____

5. People everywhere were reading novels about African American life. They also were reading poems and plays about African American life.

_____

_____

Notes for Home: Your child combined sentences by using compound subjects and objects. *Home Activity:* Challenge your child to make up sets of sentences for you to combine using compound subjects and compound objects.

Commas

A **series** is a group of items. Items in sentences can be nouns, verbs, or other words. In a sentence, commas are used to separate items in a series.

 Langston Hughes, Nella Larsen, and Zora Neale Hurston were all Harlem writers.

When you speak to, or address, a person by name, you are using a name in **direct address.** Commas are used when the name is at the beginning, in the middle, or at the end of a sentence.

Louis, have you read the biography of Langston Hughes?
No, Tanya, I haven't.
Why not, Louis?

Commas are also used in dates and addresses:

- between the day and the month: *Friday, June 4*
- between the date and the year: *Tanya was born on June 5, 1991.*
- between the city and the state: *Burlington, Vermont*
- after the street address, the city, and the zip code, if the address appears in the middle of a sentence: *She moved to 23 W. 5th St., Columbus, Ohio 43216, when she was five.*

Directions: Add commas as needed to each sentence.

1. Tanya is reading about writers painters and musicians who lived in Harlem.

2. Her favorite writers are Langston Hughes Richard Wright and Jessie Faucet.

3. Tanya what are you doing?

4. I am reading Mother.

5. I have to finish this book call Grandma and write my report.

6. Tanya's grandma lives in Marquette Michigan 49855 near a lake.

7. She was born on March 9 1942 and lived in Harlem for many years.

8. Tanya plans to do her research organize her notes and write her report.

9. Grandma have you ever read any books by Langston Hughes?

10. Yes Tanya he is one of my favorite writers.

 Notes for Home: Your child used commas to separate items in a series, with names used in direct address, in dates, and in addresses. *Home Activity:* Look through a book with your child and ask him or her to explain why commas are used as they are.

Commas

Directions: Add commas as needed to each sentence.

1. Keisha Jennifer and Otto had to choose a subject for a school report.

2. Keisha help us pick a famous writer.

3. Otto and Jennifer weren't sure if they wanted to write about an author a songwriter or a poet.

4. They knew that Langston Hughes wrote books stories poems and plays.

5. They began their research on Friday January 16.

6. Their report was due in two weeks on Friday January 30.

7. They went to the library bookstores and the school's computer lab.

8. Jennifer took lots of books home read them and returned them to the library.

9. Keisha even wrote to a library at 1185 6th Ave. New York New York 10036 to get more information.

10. The information arrived on Monday January 26.

11. Otto's mother sister and brother helped him do research on the Internet.

12. At last, the three friends finished their report on Thursday January 29.

13. They read the report to their teacher classmates and the school principal.

14. Everyone agreed it was the best report their school in Newark New Jersey had ever seen!

15. Class let's applaud these three students!

Write a Letter

Write a letter to a favorite author. List at least three of your favorite books by that author and describe some of the things you like about them. Remember to use commas in your letter.

Notes for Home: Your child used commas in a series, in direct address, and in dates and addresses. **Home Activity:** Ask your child to name three of something, such as three favorite colors. Then have him or her write the three in a list, using commas correctly.

Commas

Underline the sentence in which commas are used correctly.

1. He read many books, written in Chicago Illinois.

2. Laura, Danielle, and Sophie are going to the show.

3. Alicia are you, coming too?

Use **commas** to separate items in a **series.** Also use a comma to separate a name in **direct address** from the rest of the sentence. In a **date,** use commas between the day and the month, and between the date and the year. In an **address,** use a comma between the city and the state, and after the street address, the city, and the Zip Code if the address is in the middle of a sentence.

Directions: Add commas to each sentence as needed.

1. Andreas left Alaska on July 17 1996.

2. A book a game a rope and a box sat on the windowsill.

3. Bill do you know where your brother is?

4. Pants more socks and a shirt covered a chair.

5. Karen bring me the new blanket.

6. A bank another game and a horseshoe were on the rug.

7. His desk was dirty wobbly and messy.

8. Jeanne lives at 1002 Sue Parkway Ann Arbor MI 48103.

9. Some marbles a pencil and a sweater were under his bed.

10. José was born on October 1 1990.

Notes for Home: Your child corrected sentences by adding commas. *Home Activity:* Write a brief letter to your child, leaving out commas in dates, series, and addresses. Have your child correct the letter by adding commas where they belong.

Commas

Directions: Add commas where they are needed in these sentences.

1. Puerto Rico Jamaica and Haiti are all Caribbean islands.

2. The weather in Puerto Rico is usually warm breezy and pleasant.

3. The beaches tropical forests and water attract many tourists.

4. Children play swim and build sand castles along the beaches.

5. Puerto Rico's major products are milk eggs and coffee.

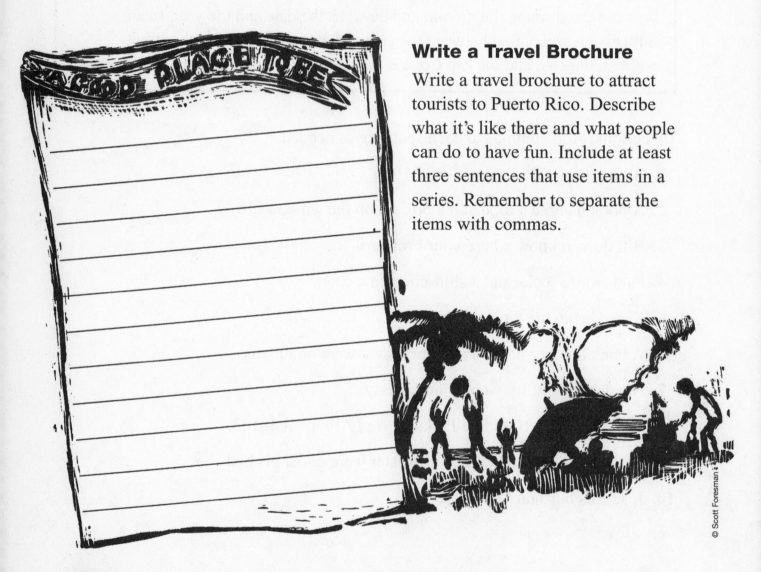

Write a Travel Brochure

Write a travel brochure to attract tourists to Puerto Rico. Describe what it's like there and what people can do to have fun. Include at least three sentences that use items in a series. Remember to separate the items with commas.

Notes for Home: Your child identified and wrote commas in a series of items in sentences. *Home Activity:* Have your child write sentences that list what he or she will do over the weekend. Remind your child to include commas between items in the list.

Name_____

Commas

REVIEW

Directions: Add a comma where needed to each sentence.

1. The typewriter was invented in 1867 and this invention changed the world.

2. The typewriter seems old-fashioned now but it was an important invention.

3. The typewriter speeded up writing and it also brought more women into offices.

4. Was the telephone invented at the same time or did it come along later?

5. Alexander Graham Bell was the inventor and the first user of the telephone and he introduced it in 1876.

6. Tape recorders may seem modern but they first appeared in 1899.

7. Did Gabriel D. Fahrenheit invent the thermometer or was it invented by Anders Celsius?

8. Actually, Galileo invented the thermometer in 1593 and Gabriel D. Fahrenheit created the mercury thermometer.

9. An alcohol thermometer was invented in 1641 but Gabriel D. Fahrenheit's use of mercury in 1714 made it more accurate.

10. Anders Celsius developed a metric scale for the thermometer in 1742 and most thermometers today show both Fahrenheit and Celsius scales.

11. If you were around before 1849 you had trouble holding things together.

12. When the safety pin appeared in 1849 life became easier.

13. "After Velcro was invented in 1948" I said, "life became easier still."

14. If you wore a turtleneck sweater you didn't need either invention.

15. "Because humans are creative" my friend said, "new inventions appear every day."

Notes for Home: Your child used commas with compound sentences and complex sentences. *Home Activity:* Dictate sentences to your child from a book or a magazine. Challenge your child to add commas where needed.

Quotations and Quotation Marks

A speaker's exact words are called a **quotation.** When you write a quotation, use **quotation marks (" ")** at the beginning and end of the speaker's exact words.

> Ben Franklin said, "Early to bed and early to rise makes a man healthy, wealthy, and wise."

Rules:
- Begin the quotation with a capital letter.
- If the quotation comes last in a sentence, use a comma to separate it from the rest of the sentence.
- If the quotation comes first, use a comma, a question mark, or an exclamation mark to separate the quotation from the rest of the sentence.
- Periods and commas at the end of quotations appear before the quotation mark.
- If the quotation is a question or an exclamation, place the question mark or exclamation mark before the quotation marks at the end of the speaker's words.

> "I like to experiment with my new science kit," said John.
> "Don't blow up the house!" his sister joked.

Directions: Rewrite each sentence, adding quotation marks.

1. Have you seen the new invention Ben made? asked Letitia.

_____

2. I haven't seen it yet, answered Thomas.

_____

3. I can't wait to see it! said Letitia.

_____

4. Thomas said, I heard it can light up a whole room!

_____

5. Should I wear my sunglasses? asked Letitia.

_____

 Notes for Home: Your child used quotation marks to set off a speaker's exact words. *Home Activity:* Look at a favorite book with your child. Help him or her find examples of quotation marks. Talk about how they are used.

Quotations and Quotation Marks

Directions: Add quotation marks and the correct punctuation to each sentence.

1. Madeleine said I'm going to try my own experiment!

2. No you're not said her teacher.

3. Why not asked Madeleine.

4. Her teacher explained You have to do a lot of research before you try an experiment.

5. I guess I better think about it carefully said Madeleine.

Directions: Write sentences on the lines below to continue the conversation between Madeleine and her teacher. Use quotation marks in each sentence.

6. _____

7. _____

8. _____

9. _____

10. _____

Write a Conversation

On a separate sheet of paper, write a conversation between two friends talking about a science experiment or an invention. Use quotation marks to show each speaker's exact words. Remember to put all punctuation that goes with the quotation *inside* the quotation marks.

Notes for Home: Your child used commas with compound sentences and complex sentences. *Home Activity:* Dictate sentences to your child from a book or a magazine. Challenge your child to add commas where needed.

Quotations and Quotation Marks

Read the sentences. Circle all the quotation marks. Underline all the periods, commas, question marks, and exclamation marks.

1. "I like to see the stars," Kirsten said.

2. "When should we look?" her brother asked.

3. Their mother called, "Come right now!"

Notice that a comma or an end mark always separates the quotation from the speaker.

Use **quotation marks** to show the exact words of a speaker. Place a comma, period, question mark, or exclamation mark just before the second quotation mark.

Directions: The exact words of the speaker are underlined. Write quotation marks where needed.

1. I found my telescope, called Kirsten.

2. Will you look at the stars tonight? asked her mother.

3. I will if the sky is clear, replied Kirsten.

4. Mars also will be in view, added her brother.

5. Her father asked, Are you excited?

6. I can't wait! cried Kirsten.

Directions: Write the correct punctuation marks in the spaces.

7. __ I'd love to travel in space __ __ exclaimed Kirsten __

8. __ Do you want to go to a certain planet __ __ asked her mother __

 Notes for Home: Your child identified and punctuated quotations. *Home Activity:* Have your child interview you and summarize your responses to his or her questions. Remind your child to use quotation marks to show the exact words you used.

© Scott Foresman 4

Quotations and Quotation Marks

Directions: Write each sentence, adding quotation marks and other correct punctuation marks where needed.

1. I found a bird's nest in this tree said Scott.

   _____

2. What kind of nest is it asked Mark.

   _____

3. The nest has blue eggs in it replied Scott.

   _____

4. Don't touch the eggs Lea pleaded.

   _____

5. I would never do that Scott said.

   _____

Directions: Write the necessary four punctuation marks in each sentence.

6. __ I've read many books about bird nests __ __ said Scott __

7. __ Can you tell us an interesting fact __ __ asked Lea __

8. Scott said happily __ __ One kind of bird doesn't build a nest __ __

9. __ What does the bird do with its eggs __ __ asked Mary __

10. __ It lays one egg on a branch and sits on it __ __ stated Scott __

11. Lea exclaimed __ __ That's really amazing __ __

Write a Conversation

On a separate sheet of paper, write a conversation between you and a friend about a bird you have read about or seen. Include quotations in your conversation.

Notes for Home: Your child wrote and punctuated quotations—the exact words of a speaker. *Home Activity:* Have your child write an imaginary conversation between himself or herself and a famous person. Remind your child to use quotation marks.

Quotations

Directions: Draw a circle around any letter that should be capitalized.
If no letters need to be capitalized, write **N** on the line.

_____ **1.** "where's the white mouse?" Jenny asked.

_____ **2.** "The white mouse?" said Jamal. "it's in its cage."

_____ **3.** "If you look," replied Jenny, "you'll see it's not there."

_____ **4.** "That's not good. where could it be?" Jamal asked.

_____ **5.** Jenny answered, "we'd better start looking for it."

Directions: Each sentence is missing a punctuation mark—a comma, a period, or a question mark. Write the mark where it is needed. Use an insert symbol (∧) if necessary.

6. " I don't see the mouse anywhere " complained Jamal.

7. Jenny replied " Well, let's keep looking. "

8. " Could one of the kids have taken it home " asked Jamal.

9. " It's possible, " said Jenny " but the teacher didn't mention it. "

10. Jamal said, " I just hope it's all right "

11. Suddenly Jamal said " What's that? "

12. " What's what " asked Jenny.

Directions: Write a sentence that uses each group of words as a quotation.

13. what's that spot of white over there

_____

14. it looks like a mouse to me

_____

15. it looks okay!

_____

Notes for Home: Your child reviewed the use of capital letters and punctuation with quotations in sentences. ***Home Activity:*** Work with your child to write a short story about a pet and its owners. Include dialogue. Have your child write out the story.

Review of Compound and Complex Sentences

A **compound sentence** contains two simple sentences. They are joined by a comma and a conjunction such as *and, but,* or *or.* The two sentences must have ideas that go together.

Two Sentences: Steve was a pet detective. He found my dog, Misty.

Compound Sentence: Steve was a pet detective, and he found my dog, Misty.

A **complex sentence** is made by combining a simple sentence with a group of words that cannot stand on its own as a sentence. The group of words is joined to the sentence with a word such as *because* or *when.*

He likes dogs, because they are usually friendly.

When he feels sad, he takes his dog for a walk.

Directions: Write whether each sentence is **compound** or **complex.**

_____ **1.** Our cat was lost, and we didn't know where to look.

_____ **2.** The detective came, and she began looking for our cat.

_____ **3.** When she found our cat, we cheered loudly.

_____ **4.** The detective was smart, and she was good at her job.

_____ **5.** Because she knew just where to look, we found our cat!

Directions: Match each group of words on the left with a group on the right to make a compound or a complex sentence. Write the letter on the line.

_____ **6.** Joe hired us to find his pet frog,

_____ **7.** We knew that the frog would be tired,

_____ **8.** We looked outside for the frog,

_____ **9.** We wanted to take a rest,

_____ **10.** When we finally found the frog,

a. and it would be hungry too.

b. and we also looked inside.

c. because it was lost.

d. Joe was happy and relieved.

e. but we knew we had to keep looking.

Notes for Home: Your child reviewed compound and complex sentences. *Home Activity:* Look at a favorite book with your child. Invite him or her to find examples of compound and complex sentences.

Review of Compound and Complex Sentences

Directions: Join the two sentences to form a compound sentence. Use *and* and a comma to combine them. Write the compound sentence on the line.

1. Being a detective is hard. It requires a lot of work.

_____

_____

2. I have a good memory. I never forget a face.

_____

_____

3. My teacher thinks I would be a good detective. Someday I might try to be one.

_____

_____

Directions: Add a simple sentence to each sentence part to form a complex sentence.

4. When I have a great idea, _____

_____

5. When I'm not sure that I'll remember my idea, _____

_____

Write a What-If Story

What would happen if you had a really great idea? Write a story about it on a separate sheet of paper. Use at least two compound and two complex sentences.

Notes for Home: Your child reviewed compound and complex sentences. ***Home Activity:*** You can form complex sentences with your child by saying: "*If I were a _____, I would . . .*" Take turns filling in the blank and completing the sentence. *(If I were a dog, I would run around all day.)*

Review of Compound and Complex Sentences

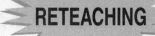

RETEACHING

Combine the sentences to form a compound sentence.

1. Reading was his favorite subject.   He read widely.

_____

Combine the groups of words to form a complex sentence.

2. We wanted to leave   because we were tired.

_____

A **compound sentence** contains two simple sentences joined by a comma and a conjunction, such as **and, but,** or **or.** The simple sentences must have ideas that go together. A **complex sentence** is made by combining a simple sentence with a group of words that cannot stand alone as a sentence.

Directions: Combine each pair of sentences to form a compound sentence. Use **and** and a comma to combine them. Write each new sentence on the line.

1. Ben lived a full life.   His achievements were many.

_____

2. His brother printed a newspaper.   Ben wrote for it.

_____

Directions: Write whether each sentence is **compound** or **complex.**

_____ **3.** Daniel missed the directions because he was late.

_____ **4.** Dori enjoyed singing, and she sang every day.

_____ **5.** When we walked outside, we noticed it was raining.

_____ **6.** We are going to Grandpa's house, and he will make us pancakes.

Notes for Home: Your child identified compound and complex sentences. *Home Activity:* Ask your child to give you an example of a compound sentence and a complex sentence. Challenge him or her to explain the differences between the two.

© Scott Foresman 4

Review of Compound and Complex Sentences

Directions: Combine each pair of word groups to make a compound or a complex sentence. Write each sentence on the lines.

1. Many cartoonists begin with a pencil outline.   A pen is used in a later step.

_____

_____

2. Movement is shown by using lines.   Speech is shown by putting words in a balloon.

_____

_____

3. After drawings are scanned into a computer   Computer operators can shade areas of the images.

_____

_____

4. The pictures can be seen on a computer screen.   They can be sent to other computers.

_____

_____

5. When the pictures are placed in a form for a newspaper page   The page is prepared for printing.

_____

_____

Notes for Home: Your child identified compound and complex sentences. *Home Activity:* Together, write a silly story about two animals. Use at least one compound sentence and one complex sentence in the story.

© Scott Foresman 4

DATE DUE

DEMCO 38-297